TRIPLE JEOPARDY
FOR THE WEST

TRIPLE JEOPARDY FOR THE WEST

Aggressive secularism, radical Islamism and multiculturalism

MICHAEL NAZIR-ALI

BLOOMSBURY

LONDON · BERLIN · NEW YORK · SYDNEY

First published in Great Britain 2012

© Michael Nazir-Ali 2012

The moral right of the author has been asserted

No part of this book may be used or reproduced in any manner whatsoever without written permission from the Publishers except in the case of brief quotations embodied in critical articles or reviews. Every reasonable effort has been made to trace copyright holders of material reproduced in this book, but if any have been inadvertently overlooked the Publishers would be glad to hear from them.

Bloomsbury Publishing Plc
50 Bedford Square
London WC1B 3DP

www.bloomsbury.com

Bloomsbury Publishing, London, Berlin, New York and Sydney

A CIP record for this book is available from the British Library.

ISBN: 978-1-4411-1347-4

10 9 8 7 6 5 4 3 2 1

Typeset by Fakenham Prepress Solutions, Fakenham, Norfolk NR21 8NN
Printed and bound in India

CONTENTS

THE POINT OF IT ALL

An introduction to what is in this book

… their dominion was taken away but their lives were lengthened for a season and a time. (Dan. 7.12)

On the face of it, aggressive secularism, radical Islamism and multiculturalism have little in common. One refuses public space to any religion and has been shown to be totalitarian in its instincts.[1] The second is also a comprehensive ideology, political, social and economic, which would not tolerate secularism or multiculturalism of any kind. The third is rooted in sometimes well-meaning but ultimately barren, and even dangerous, ideas of tolerance, a level playing field and views about equality which have been divorced from the biblical foundations of that value.

And yet they feed on one another: aggressive secularism, whilst it is hostile to all religion, sees Christianity as its main ideological rival, at least in the West, and is sometimes prepared to use the presence of other religions to marginalize the importance of Christianity in public life and in the consciousness of the nation. The legitimacy of prayers in local councils or even in Parliament, the celebration of Christian festivals, the Christian foundation of public institutions are undermined by claiming that we are a multicultural and multi-faith society. In effect, this does nothing for other faiths and makes secularity (with its own underlying assumptions) dominant. In such a situation radical Islamism is not slow to claim a place of its own and to challenge both secularity and a weakened Christianity.

Multiculturalism has arisen in this context of a weakened Christianity, especially in the public forum. Because the nation was unable to use the resources of a moral and spiritual tradition that hitherto had informed much of its common life, it tried to make sense of an emerging diversity by invoking 'thin' values such as 'tolerance', 'mutual respect' and 'opportunity' rather than full-blooded Christian ideas of hospitality, engagement, service and friendship. Should we be so surprised that the 'thin' values of public secularity have led to isolation, segregation and mutual incomprehension rather than respect and to fragmentation in national life? Once again, this has been seized upon by extremists, both Islamist and fascist, to promote their own agenda of division, hatred and conflict.

In spite of this, secularism continues to have its advocates. Senior judges continue to tell us that they sit, not under the authority of a Crown committed by oath to govern on the basis of Christian teaching, but as representing a secular, multi-faith and multicultural society. With such an understanding of their role and work, they refuse to privilege Christian beliefs and values in any way. Then there are those who, from an admittedly religious perspective, see at least certain kinds of secularism as benign and inclusive of religious concerns. The distinguished social and political commentator Tariq Modood, for example, writes of an accommodative or

moderate secularism which allows religious communities, particularly minority ones, to contribute to the building up of a pluralistic
society. The Christian ethicist and commentator Jonathan Chaplin
similarly holds that 'a variety of religious visions could supply moral
resources to sustain the basic requirements of a just, multicultural
democracy in Britain'. In the same way the Archbishop of Canterbury,
Dr Rowan Williams, commends 'procedural secularism', allowing for
a wide participation of religions and other worldviews in national
life.[2]

Multiculturalism also has its supporters, even though in recent
years its failings have been manifest and it has been repudiated by the
very 'establishment' that gave it birth. Most recently, Jonathan Chaplin
has argued for what he calls 'a Christian retrieval of multiculturalism'.
His argument is based on 'multicultural justice', i.e. a view that ideas
of justice, equity and equality do not just apply to individuals in
society but may also be relevant in dealing with different ethnic and
religious communities. Behind this is the recurrent idea that the State
is a kind of referee balancing the interests of different groups within
it and ordering their relations.[3]

It is important, I believe, at this stage to point out that plurality is
not the same thing as plural*ism,* and 'multicultural' does not necessarily mean 'multicultural*ism*'. Pluralism and multiculturalism are,
rather, two ways of dealing with the issue of diversity, ethnic and
religious, in contemporary societies. Their assumptions are often that
all cultures and religions have equal value in any particular society
and that none is to be privileged over the others but all must be
treated in the same way. Apart from the question as to whether this is
true or even possible, it hands the job of being the referee to so-called

secularity, which is deemed to have no bias or agenda of its own. In this situation, it is very important to make it clear that secularism is itself a system of belief and a worldview, and that it is not possible to have a completely neutral vantage point. The abandoning of the Judaeo-Christian tradition for secularism, 'procedural' or 'programmatic', is simply exchanging one view of the world for another. As far as the 'procedural' variety is concerned, when important issues relating to the human person or relationships are at stake, it covertly often smuggles in the values either of programmatic secularism or of Christianity. Thus, for instance, in matters such as abortion, divorce and euthanasia, ideas of radical human autonomy are in the background. On the other hand, in dealing with matters of equality, justice and freedom, Christian ideas inform the debate, even if they are not acknowledged.

We must be clear that the task of the State is more than just balancing the competing interests of different groups. It must also provide a moral vision for the common good and must be able to ground the justification of its policies, in the areas of human welfare, freedom, the justification (or not) or armed conflict, law and order etc., in a moral and spiritual tradition.

It is necessary to ask in times of national crisis and soul-searching how our constitutional and institutional arrangements contribute to shared values and a national narrative. How, for example, does our understanding of the existence and role of monarchy relate to the kind of state Britain is committed to being? Any historical narrative of the emergence of Britain as a nation will have the Christian faith, and the values that spring from it, at its heart. For better or for worse, this is simply how things are. The question is whether we wish to reaffirm and reiterate this tradition or not and, if not, what is the alternative? What else can serve as 'generative' moral and spiritual sources for the future?

It is appropriate at this point to note that affirming the Judaeo-Christian basis of British life and the institutions of the nation is *not* to endorse 'Britishness' or British culture as such, as some have done. The biblical prophets are lively in their criticism not only of the State going wrong but of injustice, oppression, greed and the idolatry which is so often identical with it. The Bible has within it, and has given us, the principle of self-criticism. This can be true of the organs of state, even the monarchy, the public cult and the established church, and even matters of foreign policy or of national security.

It is true, of course, that the differing ethnic, national and religious communities will bring their own stories as a contribution to an evolving narrative, but these need to relate, specifically in this context, to being in Britain and how their ethnic, cultural and religious narratives enable creative adjustment and accommodation to their new situation, rather than being used as an excuse for withdrawal and separation. It should be said immediately that integration with the mainstream of national life does not necessarily mean assimilation without remainder, and there are significant examples of communities, such as Jews, Huguenots and, more recently, East African Asians, who have integrated successfully but have also been able to maintain their religious and cultural distinctiveness. At the same time, the Cantle Report and others have noted that some communities do, indeed, lead segregated, parallel lives.[4] Such a situation does not have a simple, single cause and is related to community preferences themselves but also to Government and local authority policy in the areas of funding community projects, schooling, social housing and so on. What is undoubtedly the case is that extremist organizations use such isolation to further their own agenda. There is the danger that a naked public forum will let either radical Islamism or the Far Right have more influence in public life than they deserve.

Chaplin rightly points out that the multiculturalism debate has moved from race and ethnicity to religion, producing 'faith-based multiculturalism', but then he criticises me for noting and critiquing this tendency and its implications for the Christian foundations of Britain.[5] One of the things this tendency has brought about is the relative neglect of *Christian* ethnic communities, such as the Afro-Caribbean, Latin American, East European, Chinese and South Asian. How have they adapted and contributed in their new situation, and what can we learn from them?

Whatever the arguments for maintaining an established church (and there are some good ones), we should be clear that the privileged position of any church is not the same thing as the need for a moral and spiritual tradition being the basis of national life and the background for political, social and, indeed, economic decision-making and law-making. This would remain true even if there were no established church. In the wider European context the Chief Rabbi, Lord Sacks, has called for a joint Jewish and Christian effort in helping Europe recover its anchoring in the teaching and values of the Bible and thus its own soul.[6] This is precisely what is needed, and it is the burden of what follows. It should also be pointed out that the nation's capacity for embracing 'deep diversity' is enhanced by the cumulative impact of the Christian faith, including the way in which principles of self-criticism have enabled the tradition to repudiate previous temptations to coercion and to the imposition of a monolithic system. There must be no going back on that. Rather, the beliefs and values that have brought about what is best in culture need to be used for persuasion for the sake of the common good.

Not all religious traditions lead to the same results, and it is patently tendentious to compare the universal appeal of the Gospel with 'universality' which has been achieved, for example, by conquest. Some will emphasize social solidarity over personal freedom, others will not have a view of the human person as made in God's image which has led to ideas of inalienable dignity. There will be those for whom honour and shame are more fundamental than the Christian ideas of service, sacrifice and selflessness which lie behind our expectations of public service. The equality of all before the law will not be owned by all whether because of belief in social stratification, such as the caste system, or in inequalities between believer and non-believer, women and men and so on. Where there has been significant change, as in certain Hindu circles, this is because of the demonstrable influence of Christianity on matters such as caste and the dignity of women. This is sometimes recognized by leading Hindu reformers.[7]

The law, nevertheless, also needs to make room for conscience and scruple which is principled and not simply opportunistic. It is a pity that recent legislation has not adequately provided for the safeguarding of conscience. This has been characteristic of legislation in this country in the past (whether in terms of conscientious objection during war or even of the Abortion Act of 1967). There is a desperate need for such recognition of the consciences of believers, especially of those who stand in well-formed moral traditions which have themselves shaped our laws and customs. At the very least the principle of 'reasonable accommodation' should be acknowledged. That is to say, where the conscientious scruple of an employee or service provider does not hinder the employer's business or prevent a service, required by law, from being delivered, the employer or authority should respect the employee or service provider's conscience. If this principle had been in force during and after the passing of so-called equality legislation, it would have prevented much suffering and loss of employment of a number of otherwise loyal and hard-working Christians.

Under the law, religious, ethnic and other groups should find freedom to flourish, but it is problematic to know what are the 'community' needs that require state support as opposed to, and in addition to, support for persons, the family and localities. Uncritical support for 'community' activities and facilities has produced the separation and isolation against which we must now struggle. Whilst faith can have a benign influence on the person and on society, there is also a darker side to it, and society should not support anything which leads to alienation, underperformance in education, oppression of women or the teaching (and learning) of hatred for the outsider.

Britain's imperial past, like many others, is a mixed bag. There are tales here of virtue (as with the abolition of slavery), of heroism (in the discovery of lands and peoples) and of commitment to learning about the culture, language and religion of faraway people. There is also greed, exploitation and oppression of those with relatively less power. The point is that post-colonial guilt should not be allowed to dominate the policies of today's Britain. One feature of it, often to the fore, in the liberal apologetic for multiculturalism, is to justify it because of Britain's (and other European and American) colonial history. Very little, however, if anything, is said about other imperialisms, such as Ottoman in the Balkans, or Arab, after the Muslim conquest of the Christian East, of Persia, Iberia and India. The Mughals in India saw themselves as an Empire, and black slavery would not have been possible without the connivance and participation of certain Africans themselves. Let us, by all means, condemn the infliction of suffering by one human being over another, but let us not lay the blame for all the suffering in the world at the door of the West. This is both unfair and untrue.

The call for justice is well taken and long overdue, but it should be remembered that our ideas about justice are suffused by biblical ideas of equality, provision and welcome for those newly in our midst. The Prophets' condemnation of oppressing the exile and the stranger still ring in our ears. The evangelical call to hospitality has become part of custom. Our expectation of justice finds a congruence in those institutions of the state which have also emerged from that matrix of divine, natural and human law which both recognized the person as significant, and sought, under God, to order relations in society which were based on mutual responsibility.

Christians will and should argue for justice because of their beliefs and because of the common good, but it would be foolish and premature to give up on the Christian foundations of the nation which may make the achievement of such justice possible.

+Michael Nazir-Ali

January 2012

PART ONE

SOCIETY: THE STATE AND THE GOOD CITIZEN

1

Breaking faith with Britain

The rapid fragmentation of society, the emergence of isolated communities with only tenuous links to their wider context and the impact of home-gown terrorism have all led even hard-bitten, pragmatist politicians to ask questions about 'Britishness': what is at the core of British identity; how can it be reclaimed, passed on and owned by more and more people?

The answer to these questions cannot be only in terms of the 'thin' values, such as respect, tolerance, good behaviour, which are usually served up by those scratching around for something to say. In fact, the answer can only be given after rigorous investigation into the history of nationhood and of the institutions, laws, customs and values that have arisen to sustain and to enhance it. In this connection, as in the rest of Europe, it cannot be gainsaid that the very idea of a unified people under God living in a 'golden chain' of social harmony has everything to do with the arrival and flourishing of Christianity in these parts. It is impossible to imagine how else a rabble of mutually hostile tribes, fiefdoms and kingdoms could have become a nation conscious of its identity and able to make an impact on the world. In England, particularly, this consciousness goes back a long way and is reflected, for example, in a national network of care for the poor which was yet locally based in the parishes and was already in place in the sixteenth century.

In some ways, I am among the least qualified to write about such matters. There have been, and are today, many eminent people in public and academic life who have a far greater claim to reflect on these issues than I have. Perhaps my only justification for even venturing into this field is to be found in Kipling, when he said, 'What should they know of England who only England know?' It may be, then, that to understand the precise relation of the Christian faith to the public life of this nation a perspective is helpful which is both rooted in the life of this country and able to look at it from the outside.

As I survey the field, what do I see? I find, first of all, 'a descending theme' in terms of Christian influence. That is to say, I find that the systems of governance, of the rule of law, of the assumption of trust in common life, all find their inspiration in Scripture; for example in the Pauline doctrine of the godly Magistrate, and, ultimately, in the Christian doctrine of God the Holy Trinity, where you have both an ordered relationship and a mutuality of love. As Joan O'Donovan has pointed out, the notion of God's right, or God's justice, produced a network of divine, human and natural law which was the basis of a just ordering of society and also of a mutual sense of obligation 'one towards another', as we say at Prayers for the Parliament. Such a descending theme of influence continues to permeate society but is especially focused in constitutional arrangements such as the 'Queen in Parliament under God', the Queen's Speech which always ends with a prayer for Almighty God to bless the counsels of the assembled Parliament, daily prayers in Parliament, the presence of bishops in the House of Lords, the national flag, the national anthem – the list could go on. None of this should be seen as 'icing on the cake' or as interesting and tourist-friendly vestigial elements left over from the Middle Ages. They have the purpose of weaving the awareness of God into the body politic of the nation.[1]

In addition to this 'descending theme', there is also what we might call the 'ascending theme', which comes up from below to animate debate and policy-making in the institutions of state. Much of this has to do with our estimate of the human person and how that affects the business of making law and of governance. Such an estimate goes right back to the rediscovery by Europe of Aristotle – a rediscovery, incidentally, made possible by the work of largely Christian translators in the Islamic world. These translators made Aristotle, and much else besides, available to the Muslims, who used it, commented upon it and passed it on to Western Europe. One of the features of the rediscovery was a further appreciation of the human person as agent by Christian thinkers such as St Thomas Aquinas. They were driven to read the Bible in the light of Aristotle and this had several results that remain important for us today. One was the discovery of conscience. If the individual is morally and spiritually responsible before God, then we have to think also of how conscience is formed by the Word of God and the church's proclamation of it so that freedom can be exercised responsibly. Another result was the emergence of the idea that, because human persons were moral agents, their consent was needed in the business of governance. It is not enough now simply to draw on notions of God's right or justice for patterns of government. We need also the consent of the governed who have been made in God's image (a term which comes into the foreground). This dual emphasis on conscience and consent led to people being seen as citizens rather than merely as subjects.

The Reformation also had a view about governance as well as the significance of the individual that was to prove important for the future. The theme of natural rights was taken up by the Dominicans on the continent in the context of defending the freedom and the possessions of the indigenous inhabitants of the Americas. From there, it influenced prominent thinkers of the moderate Enlightenment in this country, such as John Locke, who were attempting to re-think a Christian basis for society.[2] This was also the context for the Evangelical revival in the eighteenth century. Whilst the Evangelicals drew inspiration from the Bible for their humanitarian projects, such as the abolition of slavery, universal education and humane conditions for men, women and children, the Enlightenment provided them with the intellectual tools and the moral vision of natural rights so that they could argue their case in the public sphere. It was this Evangelical–Enlightenment consensus which brought about the huge social changes of the nineteenth and early twentieth centuries and which came under sustained attack in the second half of the twentieth century.[3]

Sociologists of religion have been telling us that the process of secularization has been a very long one and, indeed, locate its origin precisely in the Enlightenment's rejection of heteronomous authority and its affirmation of autonomy. Historians, on the other hand, point out that faith flourished in industrial Britain in the nineteenth century and in the first part of the last century. Indeed, it is possible to say that it continued to prosper well into the 1950s. Was it long-term decline, then, or sudden demise? In fact, there are elements of truth in both approaches. It seems to be the case, however, that something momentous happened in the 1960s which has materially altered the scene: Christianity began to be more and more marginal to the 'public doctrine' by which the nation ordered itself, and this state of affairs has continued to the present day. Many reasons have been given for this situation. Callum Brown has argued that it was the cultural revolution of the 1960s that brought Christianity's role in society to an abrupt and catastrophic end. He notes, particularly, the part played by women in upholding piety and in passing on the faith in the home. It was the loss of this faith and piety among women that caused the steep decline in Christian observance in all sections of society. Peter Mullen and others, similarly, have traced the situation to student unrest of the 1960s that they claim was inspired by Marxism of one sort or another. The aim was to overturn what I have called the Evangelical–Enlightenment consensus so that revolution might be possible. One of the ingredients in their tactics was to encourage a social and sexual revolution so that a political one would, in due course, come about. Mullen points out that, instead of the churches resisting this phenomenon, liberal theologians and church leaders all but capitulated to the intellectual and cultural forces of the time.[4]

It is this situation that has created the moral and spiritual vacuum in which we now find ourselves. Whilst the Christian consensus was dissolved, nothing else, except perhaps endless self-indulgence, was put in its place. Happily Marxism, in its various forms, has been shown to be the philosophical, historical and economic nonsense that it always was. We are now, however, confronted by another equally serious ideology, that of radical Islamism, which also claims to be comprehensive in scope. What resources do we have to face yet another ideological battle?

The scramblings and scratchings-around of politicians and of elements in the media for 'values' which would provide ammunition in this battle are to be seen in this light. As we have seen, however, this is extremely thin gruel and hardly adequate for the task before us. Our investigation has shown us the deep and varied ways in which the beliefs, values and virtues of Great Britain have been formed by the Christian faith. The consequences of the loss of this discourse are there for all to see: the destruction of the family because of the alleged parity of different forms of life together, the loss of a father figure, especially for boys, because the role of fathers is deemed otiose, the abuse of substances (including alcohol), the loss of respect for the human person leading to horrendous and mindless attacks on people, the increasing communications-gap between generations and social classes; the list is very long.

Is it possible to restore such discourse at the heart of our common life? Some would say it is not possible. Matters have gone too far in one direction and we cannot retrace our steps. Others would be hostile to the very idea. They have constructed their lives and philosophies around the demise of Christianity as an element in public life and they would be very inconvenienced if it were to put in an appearance again. It remains the case, however, that many of the beliefs and values that we need to deal with the present situation are rooted in the Judaeo-Christian tradition. Are we to receive these as a gift, in our present circumstances, or, once again, turn our backs on them?

In the context of public discussion, and even in the case of legislation, crude utilitarianism, public approbation or revulsion (the so-called 'yuk' factor) and the counting of heads are being found to be less and less satisfactory, especially when an estimate of the human person is involved. Nor are the 'thin' values of respect, decency and fairness enough. We need something more robust. In such situations, we often find overt or covert appeals to transcendental principles enshrined in the Judaeo-Christian tradition.

When, for example, we are discussing questions of mental capacity, and whether it is ever right to regard someone as having irreversibly lost crucial indicators of being human, or issues to do with the beginning or end of life, such as abortion, embryonic stem cell research and euthanasia, transcendental principles are often invoked which derive from the Judaeo-Christian tradition. One such, which is to be found in the fundamental documents of the age, is that of inalienable dignity[5]. That is to say, the dignity of the human person cannot be taken away. It inheres in them by virtue of their personhood. The question then remains as to whether there is a human person involved in a particular situation.

I was for some years the Chairman of the Ethics and Law Committee of the Human Fertilisation and Embryology Authority, and the question that often arose was: at what point does human dignity attach to the embryo or foetus? Now, I take a developmental view of how personhood emerges in the early stages of life, but even if you take such a view, you still have to exercise the precautionary principle because you do not know exactly when there is a person. Is it at conception, implantation, or at the beginning of brain activity or the ability to feel pain? This is why the embryo is treated with special respect in legislation so that, even unknowingly, we do not violate human dignity. The notion that human beings possess dignity that can never be taken away cannot be justified in terms only of public opinion and even less of utilitarianism. It is, in fact, grounded in the biblical idea that humans have been made in the image of God and this gives them a dignity that cannot be violated or removed from them.

Equality is another leading value that we use in a just ordering of society. On the face of it, human beings are not equal: they are rich and poor, black and white, differently abled, male and female. So, what is our basis for saying they are equal? During the period of white settlement in Australia, Christian missionaries, in the face of settler opposition, again and again referred to Acts 17.26, 'Out of one blood hath he made all the nations of men', as the basis for the equality of the aboriginal peoples with the white and Asian inhabitants.[6] Equality is also then rooted in the biblical worldview and extends to the whole of humanity. It is not restricted to those who may belong to a particular faith, ideology or ethnicity.

The idea of liberation is as fundamental in the Bible as that of creation. The freeing of enslaved Israel from their captors has inspired many other captive or oppressed peoples to struggle for their freedom. Freedom, however, has not only to do with political or social liberation. It also has to do with respect for conscience. Once again, this is rooted in the insight of Reformation times that everyone had the right to read the Word of God in their own language and to be formed by it. The freedom and the responsibility of such a citizen are closely related to the development of conscience in the light of the Scriptures.

Freedom is not, of course, absolute. It is only possible in the context of the Common Good where the freedom of each has to be exercised with respect for the freedom of all. Freedom of belief, of expression, and of changing one's belief are, however, vitally important for a free society, and the onus must be on those who wish to restrict these in any way to show why this is necessary. Nor can we say that such freedoms apply in some parts of the country and of the world and not others. The rule of law must guarantee, and be seen to guarantee, such basic freedoms everywhere.

Safety from harm is certainly a leading concern in legislation today, but this should not be too narrowly conceived. It depends on the biblical idea of *shalom*, of wholeness, peace and safety, not only of the individual but of society as a whole. The debate between Lord Devlin and H. L. A. Hart of Oxford University, in the middle years of the twentieth century, was precisely about the scope of the 'safety from harm' idea. Was it limited to the individual or did it extend to vital social institutions such as the family? Devlin was clear that it must extend to the latter also, and that fiscal and social legislation should take account of this aspect of safety from harm of a nation's social capital.[7]

One final value that deserves to be mentioned is that of hospitality. It is, indeed, ironic that Britain had to cope with large numbers of people from other faiths and cultures arriving exactly at the time when there was a catastrophic loss of Christian discourse. Thus Christian hospitality that should have welcomed the new arrivals on the basis of Britain's Christian heritage, to which they would be welcome to contribute, was replaced by the new-fangled and insecurely-founded doctrine of multiculturalism. This offered 'tolerance' rather than hospitality, in some cases benign neglect rather than engagement, and an emphasis on cultural and religious distinctiveness rather than integration. As a succession of social commentators – Lord Ouseley, Sir Trevor Phillips and Ted Cantle come readily to mind – have pointed out, the result has been segregated communities and parallel lives rather than the awareness of belonging together and common citizenship which foster integration and respect for fundamental freedoms for all.

It may be worth saying here that integration does not mean assimilation. It is quite possible for people to be engaged with wider society, to be aware of common values, to speak English, and to have a sense of citizenship whilst also maintaining cultural and religious practices in terms of language, food, dress, worship and so on. The example of the Jewish and Huguenot communities, and of many more recent arrivals, gives us hope that integration and distinctiveness are not incommensurable qualities.

While some acknowledge the debt that Britain owes the Judaeo-Christian tradition, they claim also that the values derived from it are now freestanding and that they can also be derived from other worldviews. As to them being freestanding, the danger, rather, is that we are living on past capital that is showing increasing signs of being exhausted. Values and virtues by which we live require what Lesslie Newbigin called 'plausibility structures' for their continuing credibility. They cannot indefinitely exist in a vacuum. Nor can we be too sanguine that other worldviews or traditions will necessarily produce the same values or put the same emphasis on them. Radical Islamism, for example, will emphasize the solidarity of the *ummah* against the freedom of the individual. Some will give more importance to public piety, for instance, in fasting and feasting, calling to prayer, and observing prayer time than others who may wish to stress the interior aspects of the spiritual. There will be different attitudes as to the balance between social institutions and personal freedom and even on how communities should be governed. Instead of the Christian virtues of humility, service and sacrifice, there may be honour, piety, the importance of saving 'face', etc.

The assumptions and values by which we live have been formed in the crucible of the Christian faith and its aftermath, the Enlightenment. This is the result of a quite specific history and it is not at all necessary that such beliefs and values should arise in or survive in quite different contexts. To argue for the continuing importance of these is not necessarily to argue for the privileging of any church. It is quite possible to imagine a situation where there is no established church but where Christian discourse remains important for public life. For better or for worse, the United States is a good example of such a situation.

The 'Westphalian consensus' is dead. It arose for historical reasons in Europe where it was felt that, for the sake of peace, religion had to be separated from public life. Even then, the identification of religion alone as the decisive factor in the conflict was debatable. We are now, however, in a global context where we will not be able to escape the questions raised by faith for public life. The question then is not 'should faith have a role in public life?' but what kind of role? Every temptation to theocracy, on every side, must be renounced. There is no place for coercion where the relationship of religion to the state is concerned. There is room, however, for persuasion; to argue our case in terms of the common good and human flourishing and to show how it depends on our spiritual vision.

At the same time, government will have to be more and more open to religious concerns and to make room for religious conscience, as far as it is possible to do so. Religious leaders, for their part, will seek to guide their people in the light of their faith and to seek to make a contribution to public life on the same basis. The integrity and autonomy of public authority and of the law will also have to be recognized, and it would be best if religious law in its application was left to the communities and to the free obedience of their members. Public law should, however, continue to provide overarching protection for all. In the specific case of the *Shari'a*; of course, Muslims will continue to be guided by it but recognizing its jurisdiction in terms of public law is fraught with difficulties precisely as it arises from a different set of assumptions than the tradition of law here. The contradictions that emerge would be very difficult to resolve. At the same time, it should be possible for Muslims to contribute to the development of a common life by bringing the *maqāsid* or principles of the *Shari'a* to bear on the discussion. These have to do with the protection of the individual and of society and can be argued for on their own merits without attempting to align two quite different systems of law.

Christian faith has been central to the emergence of the nation and its development. We cannot really understand the nature and achievements of British society without reference to it. In a plural, multifaith and multicultural situation, it can still provide the resources for both supporting and critiquing public life in this country. We have argued that it is necessary to understand where we have come from, to guide us about where we are going and to bring us back when we wander too far from the path of national destiny.

2

On happiness

In spite of the encircling economic gloom, we are, it seems, determined to be happy.

The Government has announced that, for the first time, it will attempt to measure exactly how happy we are. Indeed, despite the difficulty of quantifying feelings, there has been a veritable industry built around this idea, ever since the king of Bhutan argued that 'Gross National Happiness' was more important than gross national product.

One of the features of the various subsequent attempts to measure our contentment levels is the difficulty in comparing different cultures and nations. The Bhutanese, for example, do not mention freedom as an important ingredient – but in Britain, it is impossible to imagine an index which does not take account of our freedom of speech and belief, which arose from the Biblical view of personhood, and of the importance of responding freely to the God who has created and shown his love for us. Many in our society resent the increasing restrictions on personal liberty; being freer to express ourselves and our beliefs would certainly improve our happiness.

Similarly, the Bhutanese place little importance on the value of work. The Judaeo-Christian worldview, however, has always seen the value and virtue of labour – indeed, it was the ethos around which the modern economy arose. More recently, the 'greed is good' philosophy was promoted because, it was claimed, it would make us prosperous individually and as a nation. In fact, it has led to historic levels of debt, both national and personal. No wonder happiness levels are low.

Rediscovering the importance of trust would certainly remove some of the anxiety and insecurity that many feel in the workplace. Rewarding honesty, hard work and commitment rather than clever manipulation of financial instruments would result in many more people feeling wanted and, therefore, happier in themselves and in their dealings with colleagues and customers.

Also, all the evidence shows that our well-being is crucially tied up with a stable family, good relationships and deep friendships. These depend on commitment – whether through marriage, the raising of children or the sustaining of friendships. Transient or needlessly broken relationships contribute much to our lack of *joie de vivre*: children miss an absent parent, while demands at work put strains even on long-standing friendships.

One way that we can regain a sense of purpose and direction is to explore our spiritual side. One of the Bible's great gifts to the world is its view of time as a progressive, forward movement. Because of this, we are not condemned to endless repetition of the same cycle, to a fatalism that believes we can change nothing, including ourselves.

In fact, the idea of changing the world for the better is at the heart of Christianity: in the Sermon on the Mount, Jesus tells us that the people who are really happy (or blessed) are those who do not live for themselves alone, but give of themselves and of their wealth to others.

The value of philanthropy is universal and cross-cultural; and Jesus also teaches that among the blessed are those who stand for what is right. It is no accident, therefore, that personal integrity is highly prized among those who have been exposed to his teaching.

In the same sermon, Jesus speaks of the happiness of those who struggle for a just and compassionate world. For our nation, happiness will mean a widespread sense that we live in a society where justice is accessible and compassion for the neediest is exercised by all sections of the community, and not left to the state alone. If we spend next year trying to make others happy, this new survey may find that we have become surprisingly happy ourselves.

3

Living in Britain today

What will a visitor to Britain see? She will notice a well-maintained physical infrastructure with (generally) good roads and a reasonable system of public transport (even if Britons complain about it). She will also quickly become aware of a social security net which aims to prevent people falling into serious poverty and which provides a comprehensive 'cradle to grave' health service. Even with the advent of the current financial crisis, there is some work available for people, and the majority enjoy a decent standard of living. In spite of threats from violent extremists, the security situation is also stable.

Closer examination, however, of the society in which she finds herself will reveal other aspects of life which will cause her concern: the constant reliance on alcohol, or other stimulants, by all sections of the population, to keep going at home or work or play will be one such. The social dysfunction of the High Street or of 'club-land' at night, especially over weekends, will be characterized by excessive consumption of alcohol, by street violence and crime, by large numbers of young girls out on their own and by young people attempting to forge relationships with very loud noise as the background and very thin social fabric to sustain them. Our visitor may well ask herself how a literate society, with a proud history and significant material and social culture, has allowed such a state of affairs to emerge and to continue.

The state of the family

One feature of the social scene that will surely strike her is the state of the family. There are all the figures, of course, which she will, no doubt, come across. For the first time since records began, there are more unmarried than married people of marriageable age. As the humanist philosopher, Brenda Almond, points out, whilst some relationships of cohabitation undoubtedly last for many years, on the whole they are more unstable than marriage partly because, in many cases, the intention is to avoid the commitment that marriage requires. Her claim is backed up by figures: the median length for cohabitation is only two years. After that, there is either marriage or a breaking up of the relationship. Of those that do not result in marriage, most break up within ten years.

Where there is a child involved, more than half break up within five years of the birth of the child. This contrasts with only 8 percent of married couples parting during this period.[1] More worryingly, even of those who marry after cohabitation, a much higher number is likely to divorce than of married people who have not cohabited. This, of course, undermines one of the main reasons given for cohabitation; that it is a preparation for marriage. Almond also refers to research that shows that, except for the most extreme cases, divorce is harmful for children, even where there is significant conflict in the marriage. Once again, this contradicts the new wisdom that divorce, in situations of conflict, is good for children – a rather convenient doctrine which allows parents to get what they want and absolves them of any guilt.[2] When children are involved, both divorce and cohabiting relationships which break down result in lone parenthood and contribute to child poverty, material, social, psychological and spiritual.

Figures and facts, such as the ones above, are produced regularly in any discussion of the malaise affecting the family. What is *not* said so often is that this state of affairs is not merely an accident, a concatenation of otherwise discrete events. In fact it is, at least partly, the result of a well-resourced social and intellectual movement, which emerged in the 1960s and is still very much in the ascendant. As I have pointed out elsewhere, Marxist philosophers such as Antonio Gramsci and Herbert Marcuse believed that the fundamental structures of society needed to be infiltrated and undermined. Marriage and family were key targets in the cause of producing non-repressive societies, which would then be ripe for revolution.[3] They have had their expositors in this country and elsewhere in the West. People like Anthony Giddens have argued that the separation of sexuality from reproduction, through artificial contraception, and of reproduction from sexuality through assisted reproduction techniques, have made sex chiefly a means to self-expression and self-fulfilment. This, in turn, has led to 'pure relationships' which are entirely subjective and do not depend on any social or legal constraints, especially in terms of how long they last. That is determined by each partner feeling that the relationship's continuance is beneficial to them.[4] This is also some of the background to Rowan Williams's criticism of those who regard heterosexual marriage as 'absolute, exclusive and ideal', in his 1989 lecture *The Body's Grace*.[5]

Whilst Gramsci and Marcuse saw the undermining of vital social institutions as a prelude to political revolution, more recent critics have seen it rather as the evolution of society away from patriarchal, heterosexual norms. This has led in this country, for example, to an end to any public doctrine of marriage and certainly to a Christian one. All relationships will increasingly be on an equal footing and no one form of the family will be privileged.[6]

In the 1990s, Cambridge University's Group for the History of Population and Social Structure and its Centre for Family Research were still presenting mounting evidence for the ubiquity and longevity of the traditional structure of the family, but by 2007 this had changed to assertions that male role models were not necessary for children and to claims that research showed that children in homosexual households were in no way disadvantaged.[7] More and more research is showing, however, that children of both sexes need healthy relationships with male and female parents for a well-rounded upbringing. Boys, for example, relate to fathers in a quite particular way. They need fathers for the development of their identity, especially in terms of appropriate patterns of masculinity. This leads to a proper self-esteem and to being able to forge good relationships with people of the same and of the opposite gender. This is in no way to neglect or to minimize the recognition due to lone parents who bring up children on their own. To *find* oneself a lone parent is one thing but to *plan for* and to *legislate for* situations where a child will not ever have a father is quite another, and yet this is exactly what the trend of recent legislation and policy has been.[8]

The results of this 'liberation' can be seen everywhere: broken families with an absent parent (usually the father), the psychological trauma of fractured relationships, children without crucial bonding with one parent (often the father) and, for boys particularly, the lack of a role model at important stages in their growing up. For children, both boys and girls, there is a vital ingredient missing which is needed in the maturing of their identities. The CIVITAS study *How Do Fathers Fit In?* shows the impact which fathers have on their children's educational progress. The Newsweek article *The Trouble with Boys* points out that the most reliable indicator of how a boy will perform in school is whether he has a father at home. Because of our misguided and misguiding 'gurus', a large number of boys are growing up without fathers. Is it any surprise then that they are lagging behind in school and are more and more exposed to the dangers of substance abuse and of being tempted into crime and street violence?[9] Dysfunctional family situations are leading to children experiencing difficulties in communication, especially across the generations, and being lonely from an early age. This itself has consequences for mental, social and spiritual well-being.

Home-made spiritualities

Alongside this rampant 'constructivism' regarding the family (or perhaps we should say deconstruction?), there is also the increasing tendency for a home-made spirituality. It was thought important that Christianity and the churches should be submitted to a 'hermeneutic of suspicion' so that their social role in providing stability for society could be questioned and weakened. In its place we have, however, either what Newman called 'the dreary hopeless irreligion'[10] or, on the other hand, a credulous *smorgasbord* of pick 'n' mix DIY which generally goes under the label of New Age Spirituality.

Whatever its justification, the privatization of religion since the Peace of Westphalia (1648) has had the twin effects of removing the grounding for the very values, such as inalienable dignity, equality and liberty, which the Enlightenment wanted to uphold, and of encouraging an unbridled pluralism. If people's beliefs were confined to the private sphere, they could believe whatever they liked. It did not matter to the body politic. When this became allied to the nineteenth-century penchant for Absolute Idealism and to a certain understanding of the *philosophia perennis*, as well as exposure to religions of Indian origin, it gave rise to movements such as Theosophy. This last claims to embody truths basic to all religions but is inspired by fundamental Hindu ideas, especially as they relate to claims that all religions teach the same truths and are all paths to the one reality.[11] It goes without saying that, as a movement, it is hostile to Christian claims of possessing a unique revelation.

The emergence of highly individualized spiritualities, which characterize our society today, has to be understood against this background: on the one hand, I am free to construct my own spiritual meaning, and, on the other, all spiritualities are at base the same and are leading to the same goal. This is also the background to talk of 'faith communities' and the like as if 'faith' was an undifferentiated something or other which manifested itself in different religious traditions. There is much confusion between the faculty for believing and the content of what is believed, between *fides qua* and *fides quae creditur.* Naturally, in such a scheme of things, it is very hard to accommodate a faith which makes universal claims based on events which can, at least to some extent, be investigated historically and which demands not only intellectual assent but also complete trust and a moral working out of its implications.[12]

Some years ago, the BBC screened a series of programmes on the spiritual situation in Britain called the *Soul of Britain.* My participation in the programme showed me that the eclipse of Christianity in this culture does not mean the demise of spirituality that is alive and well. It does mean, though, that people are willing to believe the most outlandish and bizarre superstitions so long as they do not affect the lifestyle and choices they have made for themselves. This is very far from the teaching of the Church that faith is not contrary to reason but affirms and completes it.

Both the 'long withdrawing roar' caused by the process of secularization over three centuries and the sudden loss of Christian discourse in the 1960s have brought about a spiritual and moral vacuum in society.[13] New Age and individualized spiritualities, syncretism, both overt and covert, and other phenomena have attempted to fill this vacuum, but not very successfully in the sense of providing a basis for society and working for the common good. This can mean that social and political decisions are made either on the basis of crude utilitarianism, which endangers personal dignity and liberty, or on the basis of counting heads, of determining the so-called 'yuk' factor in terms of what the public will accept.

Whilst Marxism, as an ideology, is a spent force, there is another ideology that is also comprehensive in scope, purporting to prescribe for every aspect of human life, social, economic and political, on the horizon. Like Marxism, Islamism is not monochrome and has a number of versions of itself, but the question is whether Britain, or the West in general, has the spiritual and moral resources to face yet another series of ideological battles.

'Nothing-but-ery'

As we have seen, there are some who want a thousand spiritualities to bloom; there are others, however, who are determinedly reductionist. They want to reduce everything to physical and chemical processes. The apostle of such reductionism is, of course, Richard Dawkins.

Dawkins criticizes past Christian arguments for the existence of God, such as the Argument from Design, as mechanistic, and he claims that what appears to be design is, in fact, nothing more than natural selection acting on the random mutation of germ-line genes so that changes in the organism can be passed on to offspring, and, if such changes are cumulatively advantageous in the environment, fit those offspring better for survival, thus ensuring, of course, the perpetuation of the changes themselves. For Dawkins, God is an unnecessary hypothesis, and his explanation for the survival of religion is either that it is a 'virus', which infects the mind and spreads throughout the population, or that it is a 'meme', which, on analogy with the gene, replicates itself in human cultures, leaping from brain to brain.[14]

Alister and Joanna C. McGrath have pointed out that, apart from other objections to virus or meme-theory, there is no evidence whatsoever for the existence of such entities.[15] As far as natural selection by random mutation is concerned, much turns on what is meant by 'random'. As the Cambridge palaeontologist, Simon Conway Morris, has pointed out, not everything is possible. The course of evolution is constrained not least by its physical and environmental context. That is why we see convergence in the development of organs, such as arms, legs, teeth, etc., that are similar in different species and, indeed, in like species which are widely separated.[16]

There is also the phenomenon of complexification, noted by the great Jesuit palaeontologist, Teilhard de Chardin: at both macro- and micro-levels we are faced with great complexity in organisms. One of the great challenges of our day is to account for the irreducible complexity of micro-organisms, such as the cell.[17] Although Charles Darwin was much interested in the conflict found in nature and the struggle for survival, it is important also to note the cooperation that exists within and between species. The phenomenon of symbiosis has often been noted, where plants and animals cooperate to feed, camouflage and protect one another. It is even believed that this can happen at the micro-level and may account for the structure of cells.[18]

A broadside, perhaps even more reductionist than Dawkins, has been delivered by Professor Colin Blakemore, who claims that our intentions and experiences are simply an illusory commentary on what our brains have already decided to do. This is the abolition of any belief in human agency or freedom and, in the end, of any meaning to terms like 'moral'.[19] Behind this 'nothing-but-ery' is the refusal to admit that different kinds of explanation may be appropriate at different levels of being or of social existence. The living then cannot be accounted for simply in terms of the material, nor can humanity in terms only of the biological. The search for truth, feelings of reverence, the desire to worship or to pray, moral and spiritual values cannot just be reduced to description in terms of animal behaviour or of physico-chemical processes.

Whilst Christians need to engage with claims to new knowledge, in this as in other areas, there is no denying our immediate experience of freedom and of agency. Our understanding of the world and of ourselves is not illusory nor is our freedom to act, even if it is limited and sometimes abused.[20]

Reversing the amnesia

Bishop Lesslie Newbigin used to say that one of the great differences between his life in India and his return to Britain was that in India there was always hope. No matter how dire the circumstances, how widespread the poverty or how endemic the disease, people could always form associations and committees to struggle against whatever was holding them back. Here he found a lack of hope that people could change their situation.[21]

As a well-known psychiatrist said recently, he could prescribe Prozac for people's depression but he could not give them a sense of meaning and of direction for their lives. Intellectual reductionism of the sort we have just been discussing, moral relativism combined with a desire for instant gratification, the undermining and breakdown of social structures such as families, kinship groups and natural communities, have all contributed to a disenchanted winterland from which people desperately long to be freed, so that they can live as rounded beings with friends and relatives around them in the context of a supportive community. Is there a way out or must we continue our progress towards a Hades of transient relationships, fatherless children, socially impoverished communities and a featureless flatland devoid of purpose and direction?

One of the basic tasks confronting us has to do with reversing the amnesia about their own origins and story that is so prevalent in British society today. As a teacher said to me, pupils are not taught their own history and certainly not what have been called its 'virtuous pages'. They have not been told that our systems of governance, the rule of law and trust in public and commercial life are all rooted in a Christian doctrine of God the Holy Trinity, where there is both a mutuality of love and an ordered relationship, in the Pauline doctrine of the godly magistrate and in the Decalogue (as well as Our Lord's summary of it). It is these, as Joan O'Donovan has pointed out, which led to notions of God's right or God's justice which, in turn, produced a network of divine, human and natural law as the basis for a just ordering of society and of mutual obligation.[22] Nor, on the whole, have people been shown that respect for the human person has arisen from, on the one hand, a Christian reading of Aristotle and, on the other, a reading of the Bible in the light of Aristotle. From the thirteenth century, the human person begins to be seen more and more as an agent, but a moral agent. This leads to recognition of freedom (and the gradual disappearance of slavery and serfdom until the re-emergence of the former after the discovery of the 'New World'). If people are free, they can no longer be regarded merely as subjects, even in a divinely-constituted order. They must be seen, more and more, as citizens whose conscience is respected and whose consent is required in the business of government.[23]

The Reformation also emphasized the significance of the human person and of personal freedom: how a person is accounted righteous in the sight of God, how we can live in holiness according to God's purposes and what accountability to the Supreme Being has to do with our day-to-day behaviour. The freedom to read God's Word for themselves, and in their own language, was an aspect of such teaching. It was from this matrix of medieval, Renaissance and Reformation thought that the language of 'natural rights' first emerged, interestingly in the context of the 'New World' where these were being threatened by European Colonialists bent on exploiting and enslaving the local populations (and, later on, importing slaves from Africa). The missionary Dominican bishop, Bartolomé de Las Casas, held that authentic mission meant that people should be free to respond to the Gospel, and this meant that the natural rights of 'Indian' peoples and communities had to be recognized. In doing this, Las Casas was drawing on what was happening in the University of Salamanca, and particularly on the Aquinas-inspired teaching of fellow-Dominican Francisco de Vitoria, who held that indigenous people had natural rights of ownership and self-government. From Vitoria to Locke, natural rights discourse was developed by Christian thinkers who belonged to the 'natural freedom tradition' (it has to be admitted that there were also eminent Christians who held to Aristotle's 'natural slavery' position).[24]

It is important then to recognize that the language of human rights has its origins in Christian discourse but also that it has to be held alongside Christian ideas of mutual social obligation and of a just ordering of society such that it leads to the common good. Against this, the draft of the abortive *Constitution for Europe* is glad

to acknowledge Europe's debt to the classical civilizatio
and Rome but not to Christianity, to vastly unequal ‗‗
which women and slaves were excluded from public life and where
gratuitous cruelty was part of the 'bread and circuses' provided to
keep the proletariat happy. As Professor E. A. Judge has shown, it was
early Christianity which challenged the most fundamental divisions
of ancient society: between men and women, slave and free, and Jew
and Gentile (Gal. 3.28). As later reflection reveals, for instance in the
Household Codes in Ephesians, Colossians and elsewhere, this does
not mean that such divisions do not exist but that they do not matter
in an egalitarian community.[25]

The public sphere and Christian values

Vigorous participation in public life must be a *sine qua non* for
Christians if this collective amnesia about national origins is to
be addressed. This would not just be about making an effective
Christian contribution to the difficult moral issues of the day but
also about reminding the nation of the basis of its social and political
organization and the basic assumptions which underlie, or should
underlie, moral thought and moral decision-making. The public
square cannot be left to secularity that is certainly not neutral and has
its own assumptions which need to be brought out into the open and
subjected to the same intense scrutiny as Christian ones have been.
A distinctively Christian contribution will remind the nation of its
commitment, for example, to inalienable human dignity, because all
human beings are made in God's image. Such thinking will inform

decisions made about the very beginnings of the person as well as the about the end of a person's life on earth. It will be about the dignity of those who have lost mental capacity to one extent or another and also about the treatment of those with learning difficulties. The commitment to equality will also be seen as grounded in the biblical teaching about the unity of the human race (e.g. Acts 17.26) and to liberty because of Christian tradition regarding the natural freedom which is the birthright of all, however different they may be from us. Contrary to the hypothesis of Grotius, that natural law would exist even if God did not, we have seen that fundamental values have arisen from a biblical worldview rooted in belief in divine providence. Separated from such a worldview and its nurture, it is unlikely that they will continue to flourish. They may, in fact, be replaced by authoritarian utilitarianism on the one hand, or, on the other, by public ethics based on public opinion determined by polls, focus groups and the like.[26]

The market and Christian virtues

Even in a market where the so-called 'amoral' forces of supply and demand, scarcity and surplus are at work, we cannot forget that we are moral agents and, therefore, responsible for our actions. The best of British business was often characterized by the values of responsibility, honesty, trust (my word is my bond) and hard work. They arose from a Christian vision of accountability before God, the sacred nature of work, however humble, and a sense of mutual obligation among all sections of society. Such values were accompanied by the promotion of both the 'natural' virtues of justice, moderation, prudence and courage, and the specifically theological virtues of faith, hope and love. It is not difficult to see how the abandonment of such values and virtues has led to the financial crisis in which we presently find ourselves. Once again, the chief culprit is a highly individualistic 'me' culture in which instant self-gratification is the leading value. This leads us to treat others, in our professional as well as our personal lives, as simply the means to our ends that must be achieved. To a greater or lesser extent, we are all culpable. What is needed here is an acknowledgement of our culpability, a reaffirmation of the other as a person of intrinsic value and of the common good. It is this that will lead to a recreation of social capital based on trust.

Such social capital is necessary for the rebuilding and the renewal of the financial system. This must be based on a strong moral framework that is derived from the values and virtues mentioned above. This is not to deny that people of other faiths and of none can make their own contribution to such a framework. What we must never have again is a moral vacuum that allows the worst aspects of human nature to dominate. Our duty to love our neighbour must take principled form in our life together, social, economic and political.

Persuasion not coercion

The reader will have noted by now that we are *not* advocating theocracy. There is no question at all of religion having any coercive force in the public realm. Its influence is at least twofold: it stands to remind actors in the public sphere of the formative influence and continuing importance of the Judaeo-Christian tradition in the history of this country; and it seeks to persuade, by the quality of its argument, that it is still best to ground public debate and policy in that tradition. Having said that, there must be respect for the autonomy of public authority and of public law. Religious communities of all kinds must be free to order their lives according to their tenets, and to teach individuals within them also to do so. This does not mean that the religious law of any community should be recognized as part of public law, nor does it mean that individuals and groups within any community should not have direct access to the courts for the redress of any grievances they may have.

At the same time, it is very important that legislation should have regard for conscience. This country has a fine history of respect for conscientious objection in relation to participation in armed conflict. Even the 1967 Abortion Act recognizes conscience and exempts medical personnel from participating in the termination of a pregnancy on these grounds. It would be a tragedy if the conscience of religious people does not continue to be respected, particularly in areas concerning human dignity, the structure and purpose of the family and the proper use of religious premises.[27] Churches and Christian organizations must give priority to the strengthening of marriage and the family in terms of advocacy for due recognition in public policy but also in their own programmes for marriage preparation and parenting. Indeed, there is much opportunity here for synergy between public authorities and the churches and, indeed, other faith communities.

Education and the transmission of tradition

In an important sense, the reversing of the historical amnesia which we have identified must begin in schools and other educational institutions, not only in the teaching of history itself but in how the transmission of tradition is approached as a whole. Church schools, naturally, have a vital role to play in showing how education on Christian principles can be genuinely open both to new knowledge and to the wider community. Such schools are certainly faith schools in the sense that their vocation and inspiration is Christian, but they are not faith schools in the sense that they are open to the widest possible outreach. But, of course, the agenda is too important to be left simply to church schools and other church-related institutions. Churches and Christians must bring their influence to bear wherever this is possible, whether in making suitable materials available for assemblies, in volunteers to help with assemblies and in tackling important moral issues, or through Christian teachers who are called to teach in the non-church state sector. Every opportunity must be gratefully accepted. It is perhaps worth saying, at this point, that organizations of Christian teachers should be supported, in every way, as they seek to equip their members to exercise their vocation in sometimes difficult settings.

The visibility of worship

Although there are thousands of churches in this land, some of them with a high iconic value, Christian worship is curiously invisible.

To some extent, this is a function of the weather, but there is also a mentality to shut the doors as we gather for worship. Somehow, worship should be made more visible for outsiders, whether this is by having open doors or glass doors or worshipping out of doors. It seems there is less and less Christian worship in the media. Surely there should be strong advocacy for more Christian worship to be shown on television and aired on the radio. It is important also, in this digital age, for Christian churches and organizations to have their own arrangements for transmission and broadcasting.[28]

In an age where every kind of depravity can be relatively easily viewed, the reluctance of regulators to allow adequate mainstream Christian broadcasting is very strange.

Salt or light?

There is a long tradition of the Church working 'with the grain' of society. This may be shown in its role in civic life, in chaplaincy or in the 'hatching, matching and dispatching' rites of passage. At times of celebration or of sorrow, people turn to the Church so that their feelings may be expressed through its rituals. All of this is to be welcomed because, if it is carried out with integrity, there is always an opportunity for people to hear, see or touch something of the Gospel of Jesus Christ. In an increasingly secularizing situation, however, where there can be not only indifference but hostility to the Christian faith, the Church will also have to learn how to work 'against the grain', that is, in a prophetic and not merely pastoral mode. This means that the leading metaphor changes from salt to light: instead of being the salt that seasons the whole of society, but invisibly, churches will have to be a light that cannot be hidden and which draws people to itself. If churches are to move from modelling their ministries on the salt metaphor to the light metaphor, there will have to be an emphasis on teaching and on the formation of moral and spiritual character so that churches can, indeed, be strong spiritual and moral communities in a dark age that may already be upon us.[29]

One of the ways in which the Gospel comes alive for people is through an experience of healing. From the very beginning the work of healing with prayer and anointing with oil has been an aspect of Christian mission (Mk 6.7–13, Lk. 10.9; cf. Jas 5.13–16). Basing themselves on the Eucharistic teaching of St John's Gospel (e.g. ch. 6), many Christian traditions have followed St Ignatius of Antioch in believing that the Holy Communion is a medicine of immortality (*pharmakon athanasias* – Eph 20.2) and a means of healing for body, soul and spirit. Much work of 'healing souls' goes on in The Pastor's study. It is important here to benefit from the different ways of understanding therapeutic work that exist today, but this should always be within the framework of a robustly biblical anthropology. Whether healing is physical, psychological, or in terms of relationships (sometimes it can be all three), it brings that wholeness to people which is God's will for them, opening them to the divine life and making them channels of God's love and grace.

Friendship and witness

Christians should always be willing to give an account of the hope that is in them (1 Pet. 3.15). We have seen how God has raised apologists in our midst, for example, to tackle the presuppositions of contemporary cultures and to show how the Gospel can be communicated in such contexts. Others have taken on the exaggerated claims of 'scientism' that go well beyond what science can claim for itself. Yet others have shown us how the spiritual dimension remains important for people, even if they have no connection with organized religion. No apology for the faith, no reaching out, no 'fresh expressions' of the Church, however, will be effective unless they are accompanied by genuine friendship. Bishop Azariah of Dornakal's cry, 'give us friends', at Edinburgh in 1910 can still be heard in our households and communities. More than mission or ministry, people want friends, and it is often through friendship that Christians can introduce others to the one who called his followers 'friends' (Jn 15.15).[30]

One of the main reasons why courses like Alpha, Christianity Explored, Emmaus and Credo have been so successful is that they are often held in the context of hospitality, around a meal where people can genuinely become friends. A warm welcome to church services and events, ease in following what is going on, and getting to know those who come remain crucially important, whether in a 'traditional' or 'fresh' expression of church. Routine visiting of people in their homes by pastoral teams, prayer-visiting and visiting people to prepare them for sacraments or the pastoral offices is also effective precisely because the interaction takes place in a personal or family context.

In thinking about the mission of the church, we have constantly to keep in mind both the aspect of *hospitality* and that of *embassy*. 'My house,' said Jesus, referring to Isa. 56.7 'will be called a house of prayer for all nations' (Mk 11.17). We have to make sure that, as people come to our churches, for whatever reason, they are made to feel at home.

Mission and evangelism

Mission, of course, has also to do with going out with the good news of Jesus. That means making a difference in people's lives: the poor should find resources for living in and through our 'gospelling' in the community, the excluded should be reached by our work of mercy, marriages and families should be strengthened, and broken and damaged lives should find spiritual, mental and physical healing (Isa. 6.1–2, Lk. 4.18–19).[31] As long ago as 1989, I outlined in an *Anvil* article some of the important ways in which the Church engages in mission.[32] I noted, for example, the commitment to *presence* of those from an Anglican tradition. This comes both from an instinctive sympathy for 'the religion of incarnation' and from the history of the parochial system that shows how the Church has been present in 'natural' communities for centuries. One question that arises now is how such presence is to work in 'new' kinds of communities, whether of professional or leisure networks or, indeed, among 'natural' people groups where the Gospel has not reached. The missionary tendency here has been that of *identification*, that is, of seeking to learn the language, customs and worldview of people so that the Gospel can intelligibly be shared with them. The missionary anthropologist Charles Kraft tells us that God speaks to particular groups of people in distinctive ways, attuned to their language and cultural forms, and, in Christ, he identifies completely with the human condition. Such 'receptor-oriented revelation' should also be a paradigm for our own mission.[33]

This is good as far as it goes, as long as the danger of any culture setting the agenda for Christian mission is avoided and as long as the Church does not simply capitulate to culture. Such an approach has also been criticized for being at ease with the *status quo* and of not equipping people to be prophetic within their culture and context.[34]

If presence is to be effective, and if true inculturation is to take place, there must be *dialogue* between the Church and the people amongst whom it finds itself. Such dialogue must, of course, be based on God's universal purposes as they have been disclosed to us in the Bible, but also on what has been revealed of the very nature of God the Holy Trinity. We recognize that each person is the bearer of God's image, that the Eternal Word, incarnate in Jesus Christ, illuminates the hearts and minds of all (Jn 1.9, however it is punctuated) and the Holy Spirit is the one convincing us all of God's justice, our short-comings and how God makes us right with him through Jesus Christ (Jn 16.9–11, Rom. 8.14–17). This kind of dialogue then is between the Church as a community that bears the Good News of Jesus seeking the fulfilment of God's purposes for the culture in which it finds itself, affirming all that is God-given and life-giving and questioning (and even rejecting) what is not according to God's purposes for his world as these have been revealed in Jesus Christ. Dialogue is certainly about careful listening and learning, but it is also about bearing witness, gently, graciously and boldly.[35]

Whilst the Church is to be attentive in dialogue and assiduous in rendering the Gospel in the idiom of the people, it must ever be on its guard against simply capitulating to the cultural values roundabout and even becoming a mouthpiece for contemporary culture.[36] This is why the *prophetic* aspect of mission will remain important. From time to time, the Church will need to state clearly how it understands God's will for his world, whether that is in the exercise of a proper stewardship of the gifts of creation or in calling attention to the dignity of persons, at all stages of life, or on matters of human relationships. Such prophetic activity will not be popular but it is necessary, if the Church is to be faithful to the whole of its mission.

Sometimes it is necessary not simply to say something but to *do* something: in the early church the manumission of slaves was widely regarded as an act of mercy. The movement for the abolition of the slave-trade and, later, of slavery itself in the eighteenth and nineteenth centuries was also directly influenced by Christian beliefs. Today the work of apostolic figures such as Caroline Cox in freeing enslaved boys and girls in the Sudan is not only an act of mercy but it is also taking on the principalities and powers responsible for their slavery. Work to free bonded labourers from their debt to their employers so that they can be free to work and to live wherever they like and so that their children are no longer condemned to the same lives as themselves is an exercise of Christian compassion, but it is also a political act which, as I knew from my own experience, can have costly consequences for those engaged in it.[37]

Each of these aspects of mission has to be kept in mind when we think of our own situation. Evangelism, or if you prefer evangelization (suggesting a process rather than an event), is the linchpin or, to change the metaphor, the cornerstone of all mission. Without it the other aspects of mission would be lame, but evangelization too needs these others if it is to be credible in its concern for the whole person. Indeed, some of these other mission engagements provide our opportunity for a sensitive but clear sharing of the gospel with people. Evangelism *reminds* people of who they are and how much they have fallen short of all that God has called them to be. In Jesus, who is the image (*eikōn*), of God (Col. 1.15) and his very character (Heb. 1.3), we can see how our sin has distorted and obscured God's image in us but also how God wants to put this right and to bring us to the full measure of the stature of Christ (Eph. 4.13). The proclamation of Jesus shows us how far short we have fallen of God's design for us and this leads to *repentance*, to a turning away from our wants and desires and a turning to God who has made us, loves us and wants to restore us to fellowship and friendship with him. Of course, the sharing of the Gospel shows people what they need to give up if they are to be disciples of Christ. In our culture, we have seen that the root of idolatry is self-worship which leads to greed, promiscuity, exploitation of those weaker than ourselves and a host of other evils. When we come to Christ, these have to be given up. But coming to Christ is not just about 'giving up', it is also a celebration of all that is God-given and authentic in our lives. In particular, Christ *recapitulates* or fulfils in himself all our deepest spiritual aspirations. No doubt these have to be sifted and purified, but their true nature is revealed and completed in Christ (Eph. 1.10). When we put our trust in what Christ has done in opening the way for friendship with God and reconciliation with the very source of our being, we are *reassured* about our own safety and destiny (Jn 6.35–40, 10.28, 29; Rom. 8.35–9). This is not about religious observance of good works but because we have put our trust in Christ's work for us. Of course, as the First Letter of John teaches, such inward assurance leads naturally to right belief, love of our brothers and sisters and right conduct. No wonder, evangelism or evangelization is sometimes called the crown of Christian mission.

4

What comes after multiculturalism?

Islamic radicalism did not begin with Muslim grievances over Western foreign policy in Iraq or Afghanistan. It has deep roots, going back to the thirteenth-century reformer Ibn Taimiyya, through Wahhabism to modern ideologues such as Sayyid Qutb in Egypt or Abu A'la Maududi in Pakistan. The Soviet occupation of Afghanistan gave it the cause it was looking for, and Afghanistan became the place where Muslim radicals were trained, financed and armed (often with Western assistance).

The movements that were born or renewed do not have any kind of centralized command structure, but cooperate through diffuse networks of affinity and patronage. One of their most important aims is to impose their form of Islam on countries such as Pakistan, Egypt, Malaysia and Indonesia. This may be why they were not regarded as an immediate threat to the West. Their other aims, however, include the liberation of oppressed Muslims in Palestine, Kashmir, Chechnya and elsewhere, and also the recovery of the Dar Al-Islam (or House of Islam), in its historic wholeness, including the Iberian peninsula, the Balkans and even India.

In this cause, the rest of the world, particularly the West, is Dar al-Harb (House of War). These other aims clearly bring such movements into conflict with the international community and with Western interests in particular.

So how does this dual psychology – of victimhood, but also the desire for domination – come to infect so many young Muslims in Britain? When I was here in the early 1970s, the practice of Islam was dominated by a kind of default Sufism or Islamic mysticism that was pietistic and apolitical. On my return in the late 1980s, the situation had changed radically. The change occurred because successive governments were unaware that the numerous mosques and madrassas being established across the length and breadth of this country were being staffed, more and more, with clerics who belonged to various fundamentalist movements.

There were no criteria for entry, no way of evaluating qualifications and no programme for making them aware of the culture that they were entering. Until quite recently, ministers and advisers did not realize the scale of the problem, even though it was repeatedly brought to their attention. Second, in the name of multiculturalism, mosque schools were encouraged and Muslim pupils spent up to six extra hours a day learning the Koran and Islamic tradition, as well as their own regional languages. Finally, there are the grievances. Some of these are genuine enough, but the complaint often boils down to the position that it is always right to intervene where Muslims are victims (as in Bosnia or Kosovo), and always wrong when they may be the oppressors or terrorists (as with the Taliban or in Iraq), even when their victims are also mainly Muslims.

Given the worldview that has given rise to such grievances, there can never be sufficient appeasement, and new demands will continue to be made. It is clear, therefore, that the multiculturalism beloved of our political and civic bureaucracies has not only failed to deliver peace, but is the partial cause of the present alienation of so many Muslim young people from the society in which they were born, where they have been educated and where they have lived most of their lives. The Cantle Report, in the wake of disturbances in Bradford, pointed out that housing and schools policies that favoured segregation, in the name of cultural integrity and cohesion, have had the unforeseen consequence of alienating the different religious, racial and cultural groups from one another.

A very significant number of policies will have to be rethought. In this, the Government will need expert help. There must be greater encouragement for moderate Muslim voices to be heard more clearly. All religious leaders, representing any faith, wanting to work here must be required to show that they are properly qualified, can speak English and are willing to undertake courses in adaptation to culture in this country: a number of suitable institutions offer such courses. Immigration policy should be shaped in such a way as to be able to discover whether potential immigrants have sympathy for character-istically British values and for the way of life here.

The cultural heritage of people who come here must be respected. They should be able to take pride in their language, literature, art and spiritual background. At the same time, if they are to adjust to life in this country, they should be prepared to live in mixed communities, and not on their own. Their children should attend school along with those who come from the host culture, or from other cultures and traditions. They should be willing to learn through the medium of

English and to be socially mobile, rather than 'ghetto-ized' on the basis of religion, language or culture.

Politicians keep talking about the need to teach British values so that there can be national cohesion. But what are these values, and whence do they come? The most fundamental of these has to do with the innate dignity of all human beings, with fundamental equality, with liberty and with safety from harm. Those learning such values will know how to respect the dignity of people who are quite different from them in appearance, language or belief.

They will not see themselves as superior because of their religious or cultural roots, but regard every human life as of equal worth. They will be committed to freedom of belief and of expression. They will know that their fellow citizens have the right to safety from harm and that this extends not only to individual security, but also to the safety of those institutions, such as democracy or a free press, that make liberty possible and actual.

Values, however, are not freestanding; they are deeply rooted in a vision of society. Whether we like it or not, characteristic British values arise out of the Christian faith and its vision of personal and common good. These were clarified by the Enlightenment and became the bedrock of our modern political arrangements. The Enlightenment, however, by consigning Christianity to the private sphere, also removed the basis and justification for these values in the public sphere.

It is this basis and justification that needs to be recovered if our values are to be secure, and if they are to help inculcate the virtues of generosity, loyalty, moderation and love that lead to personal fulfilment and social wellbeing.

PART TWO

RELIGION: THE THREAT OF RADICAL ISLAMISM

5

Islamic law, fundamental freedoms and social cohesion

Retrospect and prospect

The term *Sharī'a* is rooted in the general Semitic notion of a way (*shar'*) which leads to a place of safety, where there is water and sustenance for the weary traveller. In modern Arabic the word *Shāri'*, meaning a thoroughfare or main road, is also derived from the basic verb. In religious terminology it comes to mean the path that believers are to follow to reach the goal of the divine purpose being fulfilled for them. The associated term *shir'a* at first designated the customs of a people but in the Qur'ān comes to mean a law which has been given to each people (5.51). It is said explicitly of the Jewish people that they have their own law (Torah) by which to make moral and legal judgements (5.46) and, similarly, Christians are to judge by what God has revealed in the Gospel (5.50). In 42.13 it is said that The Way or religion enjoined on Muhammad is the same as the one given to Noah, Abraham, Moses and Jesus.

In its most general sense, then, *Sharī'a* is simply the Way of God, as it has been, according to the Muslim point of view, revealed to their prophet. However, both the Qur'ān and the *Hadīth* (reports of what the Prophet had said about various matters) contain a considerable number of injunctions not only about matters such as worship and pilgrimage but also the regulation of marriage and divorce, war and peace, diet, trade and a host of other matters. If Muslims were to observe them, they would have to be codified so that they could be studied and made available to those in the community who had a responsibility for their implementation. It was this need that gave rise to the discipline of *fiqh*, or codified Islamic Law. When people refer to the provisions of the *Sharī'a* on family issues, penalties, religious freedom, etc., they are often referring to such a codification. At first, the main interest was in the codification of the *'ibādāt*, that is to say, in matters such as worship, ritual, prayer, fasting and pilgrimage, where Muslims had a duty towards God. The other area of early interest was the *mu'āmalāt*, regulating the daily lives of Muslims, their social relations and matters having to do with the governance of the state and relations between states. Gradually, the codifications come to include the most varied matters including vessels for eating and drinking, the use (or not) of music, art, sport, clothing, etc., for which provision was made in minute detail.

It appears that the earliest codification was *Shī'a*, from the *Zaidī* branch of that group. This is in spite of the fact that in *Shī'a* doctrine the Imam has a continuing prerogative to pronounce on the sources of law, and the content of law, therefore, remains of necessity dynamic and fluid. It has, however, been pointed out that such a prerogative remained largely theoretical and did not affect the actual development of *fiqh*.

In about 200 years or so, most of the surviving codifications of *Sunnī* law were completed. In their work, the founders of the so-called law schools (or *madhāhib*) used the four sources of law (or the *usūl Al-fiqh*). They are the Qur'ān itself, the *Hadīth*, *qiyās*, or analogical reasoning which allowed them to transpose judgement about one set of circumstances to another, similar set, and *Ijmā'*, which was, at first, the consensus of those who had been with Muhammad but, later on, became the consensus of the early lawyers themselves. In addition to those 'roots' or 'sources' of law, there were the *furū' Al-fiqh*, or the 'branches' of the law, that is, the systematic elaboration of how the law, derived from the sources, was to be applied. This was developed from master to pupil and handed down as the tools needed for the practice of *fiqh*. *Qiyās*, or analogical reasoning, is quite a strict method for using the sources in deciding questions that arise in new situations. In addition, there is also the use of *ra'y*. At first, this was the use of the judges' own deliberation and judgement, on a particular matter, where no precedent could be found.

Gradually, however, in the *Hanafiyya* school the application of *ra'y* was allowed, even where analogical reasoning could be used in relation to the sources, if practical considerations demanded it and if the judgement suggested by such use was 'better' for the conditions in question. Such a use of opinion by the jurist is known as *istihsān*. Among the *Mālikī* also *ra'y* could be used, and is known as *istislsāh*. Here judgements suggested by a strict use of the sources of law, based on *qiyās*, can be set aside if the jurist believes that another course would benefit society more or, at least, cause less harm. By contrast, the *Hanbalīs* rejected any use of private opinion by the jurists and insisted on deducing all case law from the traditional sources. A mediating position on these issues was taken by the *Shāfi'ī* with their doctrine of *istishāb*. They held that a particular application of *Sharī'a* remains as long as it is not certain that conditions have changed. This is clearly a more conservative principle than that of *istihsān* or *istislāh* and, indeed, the founder of this school was critical of these. This tendency was further magnified in the Hanbalite *fiqh* which rejected all subjective and speculative elements and confined itself to the application of deductions based strictly on the traditional sources of law.[1] Such a strict following of the sources of law could be simply a mechanical reproduction of the school's teaching as set out by the founders and systemizers of the school or, on the other hand, it could be a creative engagement of the authoritative texts with a particular situation. As Wael Hallaq has shown, *taqlīd*, or the following of a legal precedent, need not be the blind following of a legal authority but can be, rather, the attempt to apply it to individual cases in creative ways.[2]

To a greater or lesser degree, then, there are principles of movement in the *Sunnī* law schools as well as the *Shī'a*. These certainly do not amount to *ijtihād* (that is to say, independent legal judgements based directly on the Qur'ān and the *Sunna*) *de novo* but they represent flexibility in applying the rules of a particular school of law to specific situations. In the context of present realities, such flexibility may be practically very useful. Muhammad Iqbal, the great philosopher, lawyer, politician and poet, who is regarded as the ideological founder of Pakistan, affirms the great adaptability of the *Hanafī* school but then goes on to bewail the imitative bent of its jurists, at least in the South Asian context, who work against the spirit of their own tradition. As might be expected, Iqbal regards this school as the most suitable for modern times and conditions.[3] On the other hand, a case has recently been made for using the *Mālikī* principle of *maslaha* or the public good. This requires the jurist to take account of human welfare and of the common good in reaching any decision. Such a principle may be more acceptable where the people and the scholars are traditional in outlook, as it works within the parameters of a particular school of law.[4] The great Egyptian activist and reformer, Muhammed 'Abduh, whilst advocating radical reform of the *Sharī'a*, in fact used the more conservative principle of *maslaha* in the *fatwās* he had to issue as Grand *Muftī*.[5]

Both he and Iqbal, however, were in the end ardent advocates of a new *ijtihād*, that is to say, a radical remaking of *Sharī'a* from basic principles and of the emergence of a new *ijmā'* or consensus which was suitable for modern times. Iqbal claims that the use of *ra'y* in relationship to *qiyās*, or analogical method, is already *ijtihād*. Hallaq also has pointed out that the emergence of schools of law did not mean that 'ijtihādic' activity, as he calls it, came to an end. It continued within the framework of the law schools and *mujtahids*, who could frame law simply by reference to its sources and without relying on legal precedent, continued to appear. Hallaq himself lists some from the tenth and eleventh centuries AD.[6] The late Fazlur Rahman has shown, in some detail, how the thirteenth/ fourteenth-century reformer, Ibn Taimiyya, both regarded himself, and is widely regarded as, a *mujtahid*.[7] It is, indeed, remarkable that reforming movements in Islam, both liberal and fundamental, go back to him for inspiration and direction. Iqbal, similarly, mentions the work of Sheikh Ahmad Sarhandi in criticising the prevalence of

Wahdat Al-Wujūd, or monistic Sūfism in India. Sarhandi attempted to turn Sūfīs back to Islamic orthodoxy and used his Sūfī order itself as a vehicle for his ideas far beyond the sub-continent. Because he appeared at the beginning of the second Islamic millennium, he is often known as the *Mujaddid-i-alf-i-thānī*, or the Reformer of the Second Millennium.[8] Iqbal mentions also the work of the eighteenth-century Sūfī and theologian, Shah Waliullah of Delhi, which distinguished between the eternal principles involved in prophetic teaching and the way in which the prophet embodies and applies them in the life of the particular people to whom he is sent. The former, naturally, are valid for all time and for all places, but their application can vary from place to place. It is interesting to note, in this connection, that Iqbal refers specifically to the penal law of Islam: the penalties used to enforce the principles of Islam in the seventh century cannot just be automatically transferred to other places and other ages. Account must be taken here of the state of society, the prevalence of justice and compassion in it, the extent of development as far as the judicial and correctional system is concerned and so on. In the light of the above, it is very unlikely that Iqbal (or Shāh Walīullāh, for that matter) would have agreed with the rather crude and literalistic way in which Islamic penal law was re-introduced into Pakistan in the 1980s.[9]

Drawing inspiration from modern Turkey, Iqbal began to see how *ijtihād* could be exercised not by this or that *mujtahid*, however learned, but by the representative assembly of a nation. Such an exercise of *ijtihād* would also exemplify a fresh *ijmā'* or consensus of the community. There were problems, of course. For example, would the 'lay' members of such an assembly be qualified to engage in *ijtihād* themselves or would they need 'guidance' by the *'Ulemā*. In this connection, Iqbal considers and rejects the *wilāyet-i-Faqīh* solution of the *Shī'a* already in force then and now, of course, the theological underpinning for post-revolutionary Iran. He cannot see how the *'Ulemā* can establish their claim to represent the absent Imam and his authority. He can, however, in a *Sunnī* or mixed context, see a temporary role for the *'Ulemā* as a source of information and of assistance for an assembly. For him, the lasting remedy lies in better education in the sources and principles of the *Sharī'a* for the representatives themselves. He saw the difficulties that his view would pose for Parliament in undivided India, where the majority of members would not be Muslim. This may have been one of the reasons for his demand for a separate Muslim state. He does not, however, consider what role, if any, the non-Muslim members of a Muslim-majority assembly would have in such matters.[10]

The scope for the exercise of *ijtihād* is very wide and its exercise must, in the end, lead to a radical reconstruction of *fiqh* itself. In the meantime, it can be exercised, for example, in relation to the status of women in society. The Turkish revolution led to demands for female emancipation and equality. As Colin Chapman, quoting a Muslim writer, notes, there are three great inequalities in the Islamic legal tradition: between men and women, between Muslims and non-Muslims, and between the free and the enslaved.[11] The Turkish revolutionaries were asking for equality, between men and women, in divorce, separation and inheritance. Iqbal, whilst he has sympathy with these demands, argues that in Islamic Law a woman can have the right of divorce delegated to her by her husband and that inequality in the law of inheritance is only apparent as it is a husband's duty to maintain his wife. He does not comment on the situation of single women or the vexed question of how *mahr*, or bridal dowry, is manipulated in such a way as to leave many women penniless after divorce, and without the possibility of alimony. In addition to the *talāq-i-tafwīd*, mentioned by Iqbal, there is also the possibility of a woman obtaining *khul'*, or a decree of divorce by the courts with an accompanying exchange of property or other rights. In certain circumstances, there is also the possibility of divorce by mutual agreement or *mubāra'a*. It seems, then, that there may be resources in the tradition, which the exercise of *ijtihād* could use, to bring about greater fairness in the context of divorce.[12]

A review by the Council of Islamic Ideology in Pakistan has shown the vulnerability of women under the *Hudūd* laws. A woman reporting rape, for instance, may find herself accused of adultery if she cannot fulfil the rigorous requirements for Muslim male witnesses to the rape. It is such unforeseen consequences which have led the Council to conduct a large-scale consultation on these laws and how they may be revised or even repealed. It is interesting, in this connection, to note that the consultations with scholars recognized the need for a thorough exercise of *ijtihād* in this area.[13] As we have seen, there is already much material available, from *Walīullāh* to Iqbal, on what the fruits of such an exercise might be.

Even where a strict exercise of *ijtihād* has not taken place, there have sometimes been improvements in the status of women because of a perception, for instance, that Islam encourages economically useful activity among women or that it requires their presence in representative assemblies or that access to education should not be withheld from them. Whilst the Qur'ān condemns apostasy (*ridda*) and the apostate (*murtadd*), their 'dreadful penalty' is for the life to come (e.g. Sura 16.106). There seems to be no punishment for them in this life. Against this, all the schools of *fiqh*, *Sunnī* as well as *Shī'a*, prescribe the death penalty for apostates, with the *Hanafīs* and the *Shī'a* exempting women from the extreme penalty, requiring, rather, their confinement until they have once again accepted Islam. Naturally, the disparity between the *prima facie* teaching of the Qur'ān and that of *fiqh* has to be explained. This is done in two ways: verses, such as 2.217, which speak of the futility (*habata*) of an apostate's life and work, whether in this world or the next, are interpreted as meaning that there is punishment for apostates in both this world and the next. Other passages, such as 4.88–9, are taken as the justi-fication for inflicting capital punishment on apostates. There is also evidence from the *Hadīth*, or the various collections of Muhammad's sayings and actions, that the apostate is to be put to death. This is confirmed by the *Sunna*, or the practice of Muhammad's closest companions – the only question here being about the method of execution.

The Encyclopaedia of Islam, reporting practice in the earlier part of the twentieth century, can claim that the death penalty for apostasy had been abolished in many parts of the Muslim world because of Western influence (though imprisonment, deportation and lynching by the mob remained possibilities).[14]

In the latter years of the twentieth century, however, there have been concerted moves to bring the punishment for apostasy back on to the statute books. Movements, like the *Jamā'at-i-Islāmī*, have always argued for the implementation of penalties for apostasy, as it is regarded by them as undermining the *Umma*, or the community of

Muslims, understood as a socio-political, as well as religious, entity.[15] There have been attempts, under extremist pressure, in Egypt and in Pakistan to reintroduce the death penalty for apostasy but, in both cases, the proposals have quietly been shelved because of international pressure.[16] The Iranian *Majlis* recently passed a law putting the death penalty for male apostates onto the law of the land. This would mean that judges would not have to appeal to the provisions of *Sharī'a* to sentence an apostate but could do so directly from the public law of the country. A parliamentary review body has, however, directed that the *Majlis* should reconsider its earlier decision. The Sudan has, notoriously, executed one of its leading Islamic scholars, Mahmūd Taha, on a charge of apostasy because he was advocating a thorough reform of Islam based on what he called 'abrogation in reverse', that is, he gave priority to the non-violent preaching of the Prophet at Mecca over the later conflict at Medina.[17] Many other examples can be given of attempts to bring back the traditional penalties for apostasy in a number of Islamic countries.

At the same time, there is a growing number of scholars and activists who take, as their point of departure, their claim that the Qur'ān is silent on punishment in this world for apostasy. They then go on to minimize the force of the traditions which speak of the extreme penalty for apostasy. It said, for example, that they are weakly attested as they fall under the category of *ahad gharīb* (a tradition which has a single source and only one chain of narrators) or that they are from an unreliable source, or both. Similarly, it is argued that even the *Hadīth* and the *Sunna* cannot trump the Qur'ān and that one *Hadīth* must cohere with all the others.[18] It is also claimed that the second Caliph 'Umar disliked the death penalty for apostasy and preferred imprisonment. In this, he is said to have been followed by a number of the early *fuqahā* or canon lawyers. The late Dr Zakī Badawī has traced the development of thought about *ridda* among the Egyptian '*Ulemā*. He shows how Muhammad 'Abduh himself and his disciple, Rashīd Ridā, the mentor, no less, of the *Ikhwān Al-Muslimīn* (or the Muslim Brotherhood) argued that the Qur'ān guarantees freedom of religion. He goes on to show how this idea has taken root in the thought of leading scholars at Al-Azhar (the premier place of *Sunnī* learning in the world). Typically, in this kind of thinking, the apostate is to have freedom of religion and should be treated like one who has never been a Muslim.[19] In line with such a view, an important Al-Azhar committee has recommended that an apostate should be given a whole lifetime to repent instead of the three days normally allowed in *fiqh*. These are encouraging developments, indeed, but at the same time attacks on prominent personalities, such as Naguib Mahfouz, and legal action against dissidents such as Nasr Abū-Zayd and Nawwāl Al-Sa'adāwī continue. Most recently, a young woman, Inas Rafaat As-Sa'īd Muhammad Hassan, was arrested because she had converted to Christianity. In such situations, we have to ask exactly what is the cash value of *fatwās* from even revered institutions like Al-Azhar As-Sharīf.

The crime of apostasy and its penalties apply, obviously, only to Muslims, even if only in name; the offence of *Sabb*, of insulting the Qur'ān or the Prophet of Islam, applies also to non-Muslims. Once again, there is unanimity among the lawyers that anyone who blasphemes against Muhammad is to be put to death, although *how* the execution is to be carried out varies from one authority to another. It is such agreement that led the Federal *Sharī'at* Court in Pakistan to rule that the death penalty was mandatory for blaspheming the Prophet of Islam. The so-called Blasphemy Law has caused great suffering for Christians and other non-Muslim communities and individuals in Pakistan, as well as for some Muslims. The law has become a way of settling scores and of gaining advantage in matters like property disputes. It has also seriously affected research, teaching and freedom of expression. There have been many convictions in the lower courts, though, fortunately, the higher courts have to date overturned these verdicts. In the meantime, the accused has to be held in custody (even if mainly for their own protection), the family is left destitute and the community from which the accused comes faces harassment and intimidation. Even if a person is acquitted, they are not safe from the mob, and judges who have acquitted people have been attacked and even murdered.

Again, as with apostasy, there seems to be no provision in the Qur'ān for such a draconian punishment. At the most, the Qur'ān threatens those who insult God and the Prophet with God's curse in this life and in the next and 'a humiliating punishment' (33.57). It is claimed that the execution of poets, such as Kaʿb ibn Ashraf, who had used their poetry to insult the Prophet, set a precedent for executing blasphemers. Against this, it is argued that the poets were not put to death for blasphemy but for sedition that was causing unrest in the *umma*.[20] Tradition also records that, whilst some were punished for insulting the Prophet, others were pardoned by Muhammad himself. Which of these attitudes is to prevail in Muslim communities and nations today?

From time to time, successive governments in Pakistan, realizing how the law has affected their reputation internationally, have tried to ease the force of it through various administrative and judicial measures. None of these has been wholly successful, and the law returns, again and again, to haunt the politicians and the legal community. The only real solution is to find resources in Islamic tradition itself to question the very basis of the law and thus to lead to its repeal. Pending this, it may be necessary to suspend or to abolish the death penalty altogether. In the case of blasphemy, this would still leave available other penalties for insulting people's beliefs or inciting religious hatred. Such penalties existed before the current law was promulgated and there is no evidence to suggest that they were not enough.

It is claimed that some *'Ulemā* will object to the abolition or suspension of the death penalty, as Islamic law prescribes the *lex talionis* or *qisās* for murder. The relatives of the murdered person have the right to seek life for life or, alternatively, compensation (*diya*). If the death penalty is suspended or abolished for all serious crime, how will this condition be met? It is already the case that it is the state that determines the nature of the crime and the punishment due for committing it. Personal vengeance by relatives is excluded. They can, of course, accept the *diya* in place of the killer's execution. Would it not be possible for the state, representing the *Umma* as a whole, to decide that appropriate *diya* would be paid, on analogy with criminal injuries compensation, by the state itself? It would then be for the state to decide what penalty to impose on the killer. Such questions need to be explored further, but it should be stated plainly that the current blasphemy law is neither just nor compassionate, nor, some would say, even Islamic, and should not be allowed to continue causing incalculable suffering to mostly innocent people and also tarnishing the image of Pakistan in the international community.

One of the leading features of Islamic polity is the *dhimma*. The word means protection or responsibility and, in Islamic Law, applies to those non-Muslims who accept the conditions for living under Muslim rule. This involves, *inter alia*, paying special taxes, being unable to enter military service or to serve in the higher echelons of the civil service, being able to maintain their places or worship, but not to build new ones or to repair existing ones without permission. From time to time, it has involved systemic humiliation, such as special dress, houses that are more modest than those of Muslims, not being able to ride horses but only asses or mules, and, in some cases, to pay the poll-tax or *Jizya* with accompanying ritual humiliation, such as being struck on the neck in symbolic fulfilment of Q9.29 and 47.4.[21]

There have been strikingly different assessments of the *dhimmī* situation. On the one hand, Colin Chapman, relying on Montgomery Watt, sees it as an improvement on what existed in the past and in comparison with medieval Europe.[22] On the other, the sustained work of the Egyptian-Jewish scholar, Bat Ye'Or, has shown not only the discriminatory nature of the *dhimma* but also how it has been a factor in the numerical, social and political decline of non-Muslim communities in the Muslim world. She has spoken also of a *dhimmī* 'mentality' which acknowledges, perhaps implicitly, the superiority of Muslims and seeks to accommodate to and even argue for the desirability of such hegemony. More controversially, she detects the emergence of such a mentality even in some Western dealings with resurgent and radical Islam.[23]

It is widely acknowledged that the reduction of the Jewish fort of the Khaibar and the agreement of its inhabitants to pay *kharāj* or land-tax to the early Muslim conquerors presages the rise of the *dhimma* as the Muslim armies swept across much of the ancient world. The treaty with the Christians of Najrān is another example of the way in which the *dhimma* was to develop in later years and in different locations. In addition to the Jews and Christians, it was extended to the Zoroastrians (perhaps on the basis of Q22.17) and later, as the *Chachnāmah*, or the ancient chronicle of the Muslim Conquest of the Sindh, tells us, it was further extended to include Buddhists and Hindus.[24] Many of the provisions of the *dhimma*, and, indeed, the development of *fiqh* as a whole, relates to the previously existing Byzantine Codes of Theodosius and Justinian and also to the ancient Persian provision of the *millet* system. In some respects they improve on previously existing systems – for example, in the treatment of Jews – but, in other respects they introduce innovations, such as the wearing of special dress by the *dhimmis* and the ritual humiliations they had to face in their daily life.[25] Even if it can be shown that the *dhimma* in the early days was an improvement on what had existed before the advent of Islam, and this cannot be said to be a foregone conclusion, there remain questions about how it developed and the kinds of mentality it produced both among Muslims and the subjugated peoples. Today, moreover, there are powerful voices, such as Maudūdī's and some of the *'Ulemā* of the Iranian revolution, advocating a return to the *dhimma*. Some measures pertaining to it have already been enforced, such as systems of separate electorates, laws of evidence relating to non-Muslims, marriage between Muslins and non-Muslims, etc. These developments threaten to reverse the progressive dismantling of the *dhimma* since the decrees of the Ottoman Caliph in the nineteenth century.

The *Khatt-i-Sharif* of Gulhane and the *Khatt* of Humāyūn set in train expectations of emancipation which, in turn, gave rise to various nationalisms, Arab, Turkish, Indian, etc., in the Muslim world. These nationalistic visions have become the basis for the polities of many countries in the Arab world, of Turkey, Pakistan and elsewhere. At least in the case of the Arabs, Christian Arabs played a very significant part in the articulation of Arab consciousness which, whilst recognizing the due place of Islam in Arab culture, gave considerable attention to factors such as language, history, custom and so on.[26] Islamism, in its very nature, is a rejection of these ideologies, which it sees as West-inspired accretions. In its various forms, it seeks a return to an earlier form of Islam and of Islamic polity and, very often, this means a return to the *dhimma*. Whether this should be so, even on the premises consciously adopted and propagated by the Islamists, is a question that Muslims need to answer. We have seen how the *dhimma* developed out of the Prophet of Islam's own *sunna* with respect to the Jews of the Khaibar and the Christians of Najrān. Within this same *sunna*, however, another model is available which is that of the *Sahīfat Al-Medīna* or the Constitution of Medina, promulgated after Mohammad had arrived in Medina. This includes Jews, Christians and even non-Muslim Arabs in the *umma* and guarantees their proper freedoms and rights, as well as delineating the responsibilities of each towards the others. It is true that this covenant or constitution was soon rendered obsolete by changing circumstances, but might it not serve as a model for polities in Muslim countries in which non-Muslims play an equal part as citizens rather than as *dhimmīs*?[27]

One urgent area for *'ijtihādic'* activity is that of Islamic finance. The fundamental reason why Islamic finance assumes the forms it does is, of course, the Qu'ranic prohibition on *ribā* (2.275). This is a term that occurs in a number of Semitic languages and generally denotes usury or interest, in the sense of making a profit by lending money or goods to someone who needs them. The prohibition has had a huge influence on *fiqh* as well as on piety among Muslims. Various ways of avoiding the prohibition were developed by a number of the law schools, but the modern form of Islamic finance, as it is generally experienced today, was elaborated by Maudūdī and Qutb. For them, the prohibition of *ribā* means a total ban on all interest, whether in cash or in kind. As is increasingly known, a number of 'instruments' have been developed to assist Muslims in both observing this prohibition and actively engaging in trade.[28] It seems that the main business of Islamic banks is *murābaha*. This enables a customer to make a purchase without having to take out an interest-bearing loan. The bank purchases the goods itself and then sells them to the customer on a deferred basis with a mark-up that meets the bank's operational costs, as well as having an element of profit built into the arrangements. The question is whether this is interest with just another name. Similarly, other instruments such as *mushāraka* and *mudāraba* are about the financing of ventures by entrepreneurs with the banks sharing in the profits or losses of the ventures and, at least in theory, passing these on to their own profit-and-loss account depositors. Once again, are they so very different from venture-capital schemes where a customer borrows for a specific project and the scheme shares, in a pre-agreed way, in any profits or losses? *Ijāra* is very like lease financing, and the bank's risk in owning the equipment is covered by insurance for which the client pays.[29] *Sukūk* bonds raise a different kind of problem: unlike conventional bonds they are not debt-but asset-based. That is, the bond holder shares in the underlying assets for the acquiring or developing of which the bonds have been issued. In the case of government and other strategic organizations, the question that arises is about the extent to which strategic assets may be exposed as a result of raising capital in this way.[30]

There is now growing unease in the Islamic world about conventional insurance. It is said that the uncertainty about outcomes for which insurance is taken introduces an element of gambling, that is of course forbidden by *Shari'a*. It is claimed also that, because the premium received by insurance companies is usually invested in interest-bearing ventures, Muslims cannot profit from the income produced by such ventures. Some are now proposing an Islamic form of insurance called *takāful* that is based on the concept of social solidarity. A group of persons or institutions agrees jointly to indemnify loss or damage inflicted upon any one of them out of a fund to which all contribute. The fund itself is invested in *Shari'a*-compliant ventures and any profits are distributed in accordance with pre-agreed ratios.[31]

If all interest is regarded as *ribā* and is, therefore, unlawful, the question that arises is how far 'interest-free' transactions are to be taken. If, for example, banks provide *Shari'a*-compliant products to their Muslim customers, can these be provided from funds generated conventionally, i.e. by interest-bearing activities, or will such funds also have to be generated through 'interest-free' activity? Logically, this would result in freestanding institutions which engaged only in *Shari'a*-compliant activity. This would have the effect of isolating Muslims from the mainstream of economic life in a country, and even globally. It is, of course, possible that some of those who promote such an economic system do it as yet another identity marker that distinguishes Muslims from others.

It is perhaps for these reasons that a long line of scholarly opinion, in Egypt, beginning with the great reformer Muhammad 'Abduh and continuing down to our own times and including luminaries such as Dr Tantāwī, the late Sheikh of Al-Azhar, and Sheikh 'Alī Goma'a, the present Grand Muftī, has declared that interest paid and received by banks is *not* contrary to Islam as it is not *ribā*, which is identified with usury and exploitation of the poor. The Government of Pakistan, similarly, has petitioned the courts to reverse their earlier decisions declaring all interest to be *ribā*. It has argued that there is no hard-and-fast definition of *ribā*, that in the Qur'ān it seems to refer to exploitative usury and to punitive sums being added to the original loan and, interestingly enough, that a completely 'interest-free' economy would isolate Pakistan from the global economy.[32]

If due account is taken of commentators on the Qur'ān, such as Yusuf 'Alī in 2.275, the teaching of Al-Azhar and the position of the Government of Pakistan, the case for a distinct Islamic financial system is undermined and rendered unnecessary. If legitimate interest is not *ribā* and is, therefore, permissible, there is no need for the elaborate products and superstructure created to avoid interest in all forms. In the Western world and elsewhere, it may still be possible to provide *Shari'a*-compliant products for those with scruples, but they should be regulated by the law of land and any recourse to litigation should be to the usual courts. Any recognition of *Shari'a*-related

financial and commercial law in terms of public law would be fraught
with both foreseeable and unforeseeable difficulties. As we have seen,
Muslim countries themselves have experienced serious problems in
this area and we should learn from them in this regard.

We should not imagine that Muslim-majority polities are, or
always have been, theocratic, with *Shari'a* as the only, or even the
main body of law. Whilst the *Qādīs*, or Islamic judges, have always
been appointed to administer *Shari'a* law, rulers have sometimes
limited their jurisdiction. At the same time, secular or police courts
also emerged. The temporal powers quite often took over areas like
constitutional law, international relations and law relating to conflict
between states. The *Qādīs* maintained their authority over religious
and family law but, even under the Ottomans, large areas of law were
governed by statute, or the so called *Qānūn-Nāmas*. In addition, to
such restrictions of the application of *Shari'a*, there has also been
widespread recognition of law deriving from *'ada* or *dustūr*, i.e. the
customs of a particular people or nation. This has especially been
the case in South-East Asia and East Africa, for example. In modern
times, a number of states have deliberately borrowed from European
codes of civil, criminal and even family law. The *'Ulemā* have often
resisted such borrowing as contrary to Islam but, at the same time,
they have also been involved in the modification of Islamic Law, at
least in some respects. They have done this by employing the procedural device of *maslaha*, of applying or withholding application of the
law, in terms of the public good or by constructing laws necessary for
the times through what Sir Norman Anderson used to call *talfīq* or
the creation of a 'patchwork' of law by borrowing from the different
law schools.

One of the key questions facing both Muslims themselves and the rest of the world is how Muslims will adapt to living in the context of non-Muslim polities, where they are in the minority. Such situations exist, of course, in the Western world, where Muslims have arrived through relatively recent immigration, but they exist also in the Balkans, in the Caucasus and in countries like India, Sri Lanka, Thailand and the Philippines, where they are of long standing. In Africa also, there are significant indigenous Muslim minorities in many countries. The classical division of the world into the *Dār ul-Islām* (the abode of Islam) and the *Dār ul-Harb* (or abode of conflict or war) implied, of course, that it was the obligation of Muslims to turn as much of the latter into the former as they could. This is one of the primary reasons for *jihād*. If a Muslim finds himself or herself in the *Dār ul-Harb*, it is their duty to withdraw from it. Naturally, such an uncompromising position has been impossible to maintain through the course of history, and various devices have been produced to assist Muslim communities in developing trading and political relations with their non-Muslim neighbours and those further afield. These range from the *hudna*, or a more or less temporary truce, for the sake of trade, to the recognition of certain territories being *Dār ul-Sulh* (abode of peace by agreement) or *Dār ul-Ahd* (abode of covenanted treaty). Even here, however, it is assumed at least in theory that these territories and peoples are in a tributary relationship to the Muslims. Gifts sent by them, for instance, to seal a treaty or to renew it, can be regarded as *kharāj* or tribute. This means that historically there is little by way of a truly plural doctrine of international relations and Muslim states have had to rely on fictive measures to order their relationships with non-Muslim states. It must be an urgent requirement of International Order that Muslim states are able to give reassurances that their entry into treaties internationally, regionally or bilaterally, requires permanent commitments and cannot be treated as transient arrangements.

It is widely recognized that, if Islam is to acknowledge an abiding plurality, much will turn on a reinterpretation of the notion of *jihād*. It is true that the term has come to have a number of meanings: the *Sūfīs*, for example, take the *jihād Al-Akbar*, the greater *jihād*, to be a struggle against one's meaner and weaker tendencies. Armed struggle in the cause of Islam is, for them, the lesser *jihād* or the *jihād Al-Asghar*. In the same way, Ibn Taimiyya distinguished between the *jihād Makki* and the *jihād Madanī*. The former is about persuasion through preaching, as exemplified by the Prophet at Mecca, whilst the latter is about armed conflict like the struggles of the Muslim community at Medina. He regarded each of them as important for Muslims. Later reformers, such as the Islamic socialist, ʿUbaidullāh Sindhī (d. 1944), claiming the authority of Shāh Walīullāh, took *jihād* to mean a social revolution which destroys the hegemony of the rich and powerful and the imperialism of one nation over another. In many ways, for Sindhī, *jihād* can be regarded as the Muslim response to Marxist revolution. In a strange way, and whilst disagreeing with his fundamental outlook, many contemporary *jihādists* from Kashmir to Chechnya would agree. Certainly in South Asian Islam, a consensus has been growing since the time of the nineteenth-century reformer, Sir Syed Ahmad Khan, that *jihād*, in the sense of armed struggle against an enemy, is justifiable only in self-defence and specifically when Islam is itself in danger. Thus the wahhabī-inspired *jihād* against the British in India was unlawful because the British did not wish to destroy Islam. They were, rather, its well-wishers and wanted the Muslims to develop politically, economically and socially.[33] If *jihād* can be seen very much as a defensive war and as a struggle against social evils, this would, indeed, create a new context for Muslims in the modern world. For the time being, however, we must also take account of interpretations of *jihād* which remain aggressive in intent, even if there are alleged or real grievances which are cited as the *casus belli*.[34]

Whatever the logical position may have been, it was soon recognized that a country does not become *Dār ul-Harb* until Islamic values are completely abandoned and Muslims are no longer protected. The point about values is an important one, since integration depends not only on sharing a language, for example, but also on at least some values and aspirations. One of Sir Syed Ahmad Khan's contemporaries, Deputy Nazīr Ahmad, urged Indian Muslims to respect the laws of British India because they promoted the underlying values of Islam.[35] Even Muhammad Iqbal, in an early article, describes the British Empire as 'the greatest Muhammadan Empire in the world' because it embodies within it vital Islamic principles such as freedom of expression, rule of law, democracy, etc.[36]

In present-day Western contexts, Muslims will, of course, like anyone else, have freedom to practise and to propagate their faith. Their religious leaders, moreover, should be free to guide them according to the tenets of the faith and it is recognized that this includes the *Sharī'a* as codified by the various schools of law, with their differences and similarities. We must also expect that Muslims will seek to influence public policy in accordance with the teachings of Islam. There is, however, another side to the coin. The autonomy of public law must be upheld. In most Western contexts this is derived from the Judaeo-Christian tradition, as interpreted and clarified by aspects of the Enlightenment. The *Sharī'a*, even if influenced by the laws of Byzantine, is actually founded on quite different assumptions. Its recognition or incorporation into public law could cause not only confusion but an undermining of fundamental assumptions. Family law, for example, is often mooted as an area of Islamic Law that might, somehow, be recognized by public law in the West. But what would be the consequences? We have noted the inequality of women in the context of divorce. Similar questions would arise in terms of custody of children, laws of inheritance and of evidence, monogamy and polygamy and so on. As we have said already, Muslims should be free to order their lives, including their family lives, according to Islamic teachings. If, however, any question arises about the funda-mental rights and responsibilities of a citizen or a resident, there must be free access to the courts for such matters to be settled in accordance with the law of the land. The possibility of groups, like women or young people, being coerced into accepting the decisions of so-called 'councils' or 'tribunals' has to be carefully monitored. Also it should not be possible for the structures of any religion to deal with matters where a crime may have been committed; domestic violence and rape come to mind. We have noted already the difficulties of Islamic finance in Muslim countries, let alone in the West. Once again, Muslims should be free to comply with *Sharī'a*, and financial institutions can offer products that Muslims judge to be so compliant, but any dispute must be settled according to the commercial and financial law of the land. What else can we say in this regard? Whilst the autonomy and integrity of public law is to be affirmed, governments and parliaments have also to recognize the importance of conscience for believers. There is a long and varied history as to the extent of such recognition, but if the needs of legislation are to be balanced by respect for the beliefs of people, there will have to be increasing provision for conscience based on religious or other belief. In particular, this will affect issues about participation in armed conflict, the status of the unborn foetus at different stages of development, euthanasia or assisted suicide, the nature and structure of family life, as well as the understanding and portrayal of human sexuality.

While the incorporation or recognition of *Sharī'a* into the public law of states or of groups of states (such as the EU) cannot be recommended, Muslims should be free, of course, to bring to bear upon public discussion the values of *Sharī'a* as exemplified, for instance, in the *maqāsid*. Both Iqbal and Tāriq Ramadān, relying on the mediaeval Spanish jurist Imām Shātibī, list these *maqāsid*, or principal objectives, which are to be protected and implemented in any society. These have to do with *dīn* (belief, religion or worldview), *nafs* (the person), *'aql* (the mind), *nasl* (everything connected with the propagation of humanity) and *māl* (or property). Some add *'izza* or dignity to this list. A contribution to public discussion, based on such principles, must be possible and would be welcome without requiring, in any way, an alignment of quite different systems of law.[37]

We have considered then the origins of *Sharī'a* and its development, as well as its effects on the lives of ordinary people and, in particular, on those of non-Muslims who came, for one reason or another, within the orbit of Islam. We have seen also how *Sharī'a* has influenced relations between Muslim and non-Muslim states and the implications of this for world order today. We have looked at principles of development in the various schools of law and how this could assist Muslims in addressing the opportunities and problems of the contemporary world. We have examined various aspects of Islamic law, for example, family law, Islamic finance, the penal laws and *jihād*, and considered how some Muslim scholars have dealt with difficulties which arise in their implementation. Finally, we have asked how all of this relates to Muslims living in largely non-Muslim societies, including those in the Western world. We have asked how they can freely practise their faith but also how the integrity of public law and of the institutions of state can be maintained, even as Muslims and others seek to make a contribution to public discussion and debate. We have particularly noted the problem of the *Sharī'a* in relation to such a contribution with both opportunities and limitations as to its use. The debate will, no doubt, continue. What is needed, more and more, is good scholarship, both Muslim and non-Muslim, in the areas outlined in this chapter. We hope it will be forthcoming.

6

Behind and beyond 9/11

Ten years on from the ghastly atrocity of 9/11, and all that followed it, it is worth asking about 'the stagnant and fetid waters' that have given birth to terrorism on such a vast and well-organized scale. Commentators have, again and again, drawn attention to the seething, and growing, resentment in the Muslim world at the dominance of the West, the experience of colonialism, the creation of Israel, the Kashmir dispute and, of course, the *casus belli* of so much, the Soviet invasion of Afghanistan.

This resentment, however, has not just been the usual one of the weaker against the stronger or of the subjugated against the oppressor. It has also been informed by a worldview which expects 'manifest victory' for Islam, has not been reconciled to lands 'lost' to Islam, whether India, the Iberian peninsula or, indeed, Palestine, seeks the restoration of the Caliphate and the abolition of the nation-state in the cause of a united *Ummah* or Islamic nation. It should be noted that the much-mentioned 'grievances' felt, especially by young Muslims, are not freestanding but are related to the perceived failure of a worldview.

Resentment in itself is not enough, even if it is supported by an unfulfilled worldview, to lead to extremism and thence to terrorism. What has happened, rather, is that there has been a succession of movements and leaders who have turned the worldview and anger into ideology. In the Sunni world both Sayyid Qutb and Maulana Maududi in South Asia were able to initiate a comprehensive ideological system, political, economic, social and religious, based on their reading of the fundamental sources of Islam, the Qur'an and the Sunnah of Islam's prophet. Such a system provided not only for an Islamic state, as an intermediate step on the way to Pan-Islam, but, in due course, it was to provide the framework for an international movement of Islamist extremism some of which has led to terror not only in the non-Muslim world but against fellow Muslims who have not agreed with the manifestos of these ideologies. Meanwhile, in Shī'a Iran, the doctrine of *wilayet-i-Faqih,* i.e. the rule of experts in the Sharī'a, led not only to the Islamic Revolution there but also its export to countries like Lebanon. The Iranian experiment has changed completely how the Shī'a are viewed in the world of Islam, whether in Iraq, Bahrain or even Saudi Arabia.

The emergence of Islamic ideology, Sunni or Shī'a, has led to the rapid islamification of nearly every Muslim community. Indonesian or Malay Islam, for example, which sat at ease with the Hindu and animistic heritage of people, has quite quickly been transformed into recognizable orthodoxy. Even though Sufism, or mystical Islam, has been influential in countries like Pakistan or Egypt for centuries, the public face of Islam increasingly resembles a Wahhabi-Salafi profile. One of the effects of this process has been the revival of the teaching of suspicion and of hate directed against Jews, Christians and other non-Muslims. In some situations, this has been disseminated through textbooks in various subjects, and other aspects of the educational system. The increasing and widespread radicalization of the madrassas and seminaries has meant that newly-emerging religious leaders are themselves immersed in such ideological propaganda. The mass media, and particularly new technology, has also contributed not a little, with the ether being dominated by ideological rather than moderate Islam.

The net result of all this has been a growing change in the mind-set and expectations of large sections of the population who are encouraged to see bombings, assassinations and other kinds of terrorist activity as being in the cause of liberation for oppressed Muslims, as vengeance for past wrongs and even as the victory for Islam which Muslims should expect. At the same time, 9/11 and other acts of terror have had a profound influence on the American and European psyche. It is not an exaggeration to think of it as a traumatization. The non-Western is seen less and less as 'the exotic' and the 'ethnic' which should be investigated and sampled, and more and more as a threat to be avoided and, if necessary, repelled.

In such a highly polarized situation, what should be a properly Christian approach? We must, first of all, attempt to distinguish between Muslims, Islam and Islamist ideology. We can never lose sight of God's love for Muslims, as for all of his creation, and of our obligation to love them as well. Although, as Christians, we will not agree with everything in the faith of Islam, we can study it with profit to better understand our neighbour and to be able to converse with our Muslim friends, to witness more effectively to them of God's love for them revealed in Jesus Christ and to seek to serve them in the name of Jesus.

Islamist ideology, however, may need to be opposed if, for example, it seeks to reduce freedom of belief or expression, or the freedom to change our beliefs. Christians will also wish to defend freedom of movement and of opportunity for women and girls, and to resist punishments that demean the human person, are cruel and do not have rehabilitation and reformation, as well as retribution, included in their overall aim. Although they will want an appropriate role for the spiritual dimension in public life, they will oppose what is coercive and theocratic and promote what is persuasive and democratic. Alongside this, they will want protection for fundamental freedoms and for the rule of law.

Although we need carefully to distinguish between Muslims, Islam and Islamism, we must also recognize that there is considerable overlap here. A devout and pietistic Muslim can be influenced by extremist ideology, and Islamism certainly uses much in the fundamentals of Islam to argue its case.

In witnessing to Muslims, how far can we work with 'the logic of Islam' and when do we have to be not only counter-cultural but also counter-theological? How far can we affirm what the Qur'an teaches, for instance, about Jesus, and when do we need to challenge Islam on its doctrine of God, sin, salvation and grace? Dialogue with moderate Muslims is always a pleasure but we have to be realistic in asking whether it will be able to deliver on the hopes invested in it. Any dialogue should avoid being 'kissy-kissy' and ask tough questions about freedom, integration and equality.

Islamism has brought particular hardship, discrimination and persecution for many non-Muslim communities in the Islamic world and even for many Muslims. One aspect of Christian ministry that has come greatly to the fore is that of advocacy; of being a voice for the voiceless and of support for the persecuted church. Christians also need to be at the cutting edge in the encouragement of all-round and broadly-based education and of investment that benefits small businesses. Microfinance's track-record in reducing poverty, encouraging business and providing employment must be part of any strategy to reduce extremist influence. Why, then, are Christian microfinance institutions so reluctant to get involved in the Islamic world? Is it because the risk is greater? That may be, but the rewards may also be commensurately higher.

The best protection for the West from terrorism is the encouraging and the establishing of freedom in Muslim countries together with democracy and the rule of law. Narrow self-interest should not lead us to abandon the women and children of Afghanistan, the Christians and Ahmadiyya of Pakistan or the Baha'is of Iran to their fate. If we do this, we can be sure that our turn will also surely come.

7

We must not abandon the world to extreme Islamism

Not since the demise of Marxism has the world been faced with a comprehensive political, social and economic ideology determined, by force if necessary, to achieve hegemony over large parts of the world. I mean, of course, the rise of radical Islamism, in its various manifestations, with its claim to be the only authentic interpretation of Islam. I am aware that there are many moderate Muslims who reject such an interpretation of their faith and, indeed, there are secular forces in the Muslim world prepared to resist such programmatic extremism. We should not, however, underestimate its capacity for disruption and destruction and its desire to remake the world in its own image.

In the face of such an ideology, the international community must not lose its nerve. Any withdrawal from a political, military and even intellectual engagement will be seen as capitulation. Instead of leading to containment, it will only encourage even greater attempts at the expansion of power and influence of movements connected with this ideology. This has already caused and will continue to cause immense suffering to those who do not fit in with an Islamist worldview, including minorities of various kinds, emancipated women and Muslims with views different from those of the extremists. The independence of nations, the autonomy of communities, traditional devotional practices (such as that associated with Sufism) and 'deviations' from the prescribed orthodoxy will all be threatened, even with regard to their very existence.

It is true that this ideology, and the movements associated with it, thrive on the grievances, sometimes genuine, which Muslims have whether in Israel/Palestine, Kashmir, Chechnya or the Balkans. Let there be no mistake, however, that the ideology exists not because of such grievances but because of particular interpretations of Islam and what follows from them. There is a desire to purify the *Dār-ul-Islām* (or the House of Islam) of all infidel influence and corruption. This means that the role of women must be greatly restricted, that non-Muslims must accept the inferior status of *dhimmi* (rather than that of fellow-citizens) if they are to survive at all, and that even Muslim males must behave according to the dictates of the guardians of the ideology. The non-Muslim world (or the *Dār-ul-Harb*, the Abode of War) must be brought within the ideologues' sphere of influence whether through persuasion, accommodation by others of the extremists' agenda or the fear of armed conflict. The frustration of such objectives can become a 'grievance', and so the cycle continues.

The *Jihād*, for these ideologies, cannot have the meaning of self-defence, which so many moderates claim for it. It must extend not only to the recovery of the 'Muslim lands' of Palestine, India, the

Iberian peninsula, parts of the Far East and Central Asia and, indeed, many areas in sub-Saharan Africa, but further than that so that, either through the *da'wa* (the invitation to accept this version of Islam) or political and military means, more and more of the *Dār-ul-Harb* will become the *Dār-ul-Islām*. The fact that many Muslims do not share these aspirations and may reject them should not blind us to the reality that these ideologies do have them and are prepared to act on them.

The West's involvement (particularly that of Britain and America) in Afghanistan and to some extent also in Iraq must be seen in the light of what has been said above. There should be no facile optimism that *Al-Qā'ida* has been disabled and does not any longer pose a credible threat to Western or other countries. It is perfectly possible to re-grow *Al-Qā'ida* into a potent force given the right conditions. It is also the case that the ideology associated with the movement is producing mutant groups like *Al-Shabāb* in Somalia and elsewhere. Any abandonment of Afghanistan, at this stage, will create *exactly* the kind of chaos in which these movements flourish. It will, once again, bring about the conditions where the *Tālibān* and its even worse allies will, once again, not only return the country to the darkest night but also remove any incentive for Pakistan to engage with its own extremist groups, at least in the border areas. *Al-Qā'ida* and its allies will recover their safe haven where they can regroup and plan whatever further atrocities they have in mind for the free world. Even in other parts of Pakistan, those extremist groups which were created by elements in the Pakistani military's intelligence services to infil-trate India-held Kashmir will see this as an opportunity to consolidate themselves and to engage in activities not only against India but more widely and, indeed, against the still-fragile democratic Government of Pakistan. Not only will *Al-Qā'ida* seek to acquire again a capacity to attack Western and other targets, but fresh oxygen will be given to those groups that train people for terrorist activity on both Afghan and Pakistan soil. It is well known, of course, that their training and activity is not limited to South and Central Asia but that they are very capable of exporting extremism and its allied terrorism by radicalizing vulnerable young Muslims in the West and using them in their own country. It has been shown beyond doubt that Britain is particularly exposed in this aspect of the matter.

It is vital that people in the West begin to appreciate that, in a globalized and highly mobile world, their interests are not confined to their territorial borders and that 'minding their doorsteps' is not enough. In today's world, it would be foolish to be 'a little Englander' or a 'Monroe American'. Western interests have to be defended globally. Usually, this happens diplomatically and through negotiation, whether political or commercial. From time to time, however, the protection of Western interests acquires a 'defence' or 'military' dimension. It is true that, through alliances, agreements and treaties, enemies can sometimes be deterred and interests protected. Only occasionally will the defence of such interests require armed intervention. When it is required, however, there should be no flinching from the focused effort, expenditure and, indeed, sacrifice which may be needed.

In the past, the Christian 'just war' tradition provided the moral criteria as to whether a conventional interstate conflict was justified or not. Now that most such conflicts are likely to be non-conventional and will be undertaken to prevent genocide or to frustrate the attempts of terrorists to perpetrate atrocities or to provide regional security, can this tradition still provide the necessary criteria? I believe it can. It can certainly ask whether the intention is right and whether armed action is being considered as a last resort. For example, is the intention to remove palpable evil or merely to promote the extension of one's advantage over others? Is there proper authority? This could be international authority, such as the UN, or the authority of a widely-based regional alliance or, indeed, it could be the authority of a nation-state, acting in self-defence, to repel or to pre-empt an attack on it. What about proper proportionality? This is much more difficult to judge: will the evil caused by the intervention exceed the evil it is seeking to remove? Here judgements need to be made not only about the *immediate* evil being caused but also the scale of possible harm, if the evil is left unchecked.

Similarly, in the conduct of hostilities, questions about the protection of non-combatants, about proportionality and the treatment of prisoners have to be asked, even if it is acknowledged that terrorists sometimes deliberately use civilians as a shield for their atrocities and do not recognize mutual obligation. 'Winning the peace' is now widely recognized as a necessary accompaniment to a conflict that may be justified. The rebuilding of a country, the restoration of power and water supplies, the maintenance of law and order are all goods that can be expected in the event of success in such non-conventional types of conflict, as they previously were in more conventional situations. Failure to deliver will certainly result in obscuring the moral case for the action. It may also have adverse political and social consequences. It would be terrible, for example, if Afghanistan were to be left in the ruins in which the West found it. The efforts, therefore, in physical and social reconstruction, in the provision of education, opportunity and employment, are as vital as efforts to provide effective security. Such efforts are praiseworthy if carried out by the armed forces and delivered on a bilateral basis. In an environment, however, where the armed services are under tremendous pressure to deliver on basic security and where there is rampant corruption in the apparatus of state, surely it is vital to involve Non-Governmental Organizations, including faith-based ones, in ways which respect their autonomy and do not compromise their integrity and credibility. There must certainly be joined-up thinking about objectives, but this does not mean that agencies should not have a certain amount of independence of action within a common framework.

Religious leaders are not politicians, nor are they military officers. Their task is not to decide when to undertake a particular mission of this kind and how it should be conducted. Their role is the much more modest one of praying and working for peace, of always asking whether any armed action being contemplated is a last resort and, in the end, reminding ministers and generals of the moral criteria which must be used in their decision-making and in their operations. Naturally, there will be conflicts where the actions of one side or another or both will be characterized by injustice, cruelty or oppression. Such actions will need to be denounced by all who affirm basic human values, and religious leaders will be among them, but they should not seek to usurp what properly belongs to others. Rather, they should seek to pray, to guide, to warn and to encourage.

It is earnestly to be hoped that our decision-makers have, indeed, taken these moral considerations into account in the conflict in South and Central Asia. If so, what should be the objectives of Western involvement in this part of the world? They must include preventing Afghanistan and, now more and more, Pakistan from becoming a viable base for extremist organizations bent on waging *Jihād* against the West, its global interests and its allies. We should not forget that their aim is also to destabilize and if possible, overthrow moderate governments, of whatever shade of politics, in the Islamic world itself. Never again should this area be allowed to become a base for the planning and execution of terrorist attacks in the West and elsewhere. It should be made impossible for the so-called 'madrassas' to train young people from the West in terrorist activity against their own country and people. These must be the basic aims of involvement. The achievement of these aims depends very much on closely coordinated policy and action between the forces in Afghanistan and the Pakistan Army. It must be understood clearly that the problems in Afghanistan will not be resolved if similar issues are not addressed on the other side of the border. I am glad this is beginning to happen but there is a long way to go. It is perfectly reasonable to ask what Pakistan is doing, not only with regard to Pakistani *Tālibān* and other home-grown *Jihādi* groups, but against *Al-Qā'ida* itself.

It must be a legitimate aim of the involvement to protect the people of Afghanistan and Pakistan from the barbarity of the extremists. What the *Tālibān* did in Afghanistan, when they were in power, is too well known to need repetition. During their short-lived occupation, however, of the beautiful valley and people of Swat in North West Pakistan, one of their 'signatures' was the blowing up of a girls' school that had been run by Christian nuns largely for the benefit of Muslim pupils and parents. It will not say much for a Western commitment to fundamental freedoms and basic human rights if women, girls and non-Muslims are consigned to virtual captivity just because electorates in the West are perceived not to have the stomach for an extended conflict. The result of this intervention must be the empowerment of such groups and they cannot again be left at the mercy of extremists.

One of the reasons why so many in the population cannot cope with the casualties in the conflict is that there is no longer a common narrative within which people can place such tragedies and which can help them in making sense of the loss. A 'me' culture of personal fulfilment and gratification leaves no room for service, selflessness and sacrifice. Although the USA is facing many of the pressures being faced by Britain, it is instructive to see how, in many cases, the Judaeo-Christian tradition is still, if not intact, at least surviving in the USA and how it does provide a framework for making sense of loss.

The other reason which is given most often for withdrawing from the conflict is that it is alienating Muslim opinion. We have seen already that the extremist agenda is not caused by various 'grievances' in the Muslim world, but it does feed on them. Generally speaking, Muslims have welcomed UN- or NATO-led military interventions, as in Bosnia or Kosovo, when they have been undertaken to protect Muslim communities at risk. I cannot see, however, why such interventions are acceptable when Muslims are the oppressed party but unacceptable when it may be Muslims who are the oppressors (often of fellow-Muslims). We cannot have double standards here and, if armed intervention is to be allowed at all, there must be commonly-agreed criteria for it, regardless of who it may protect or against whom it may be directed. One element in inter-faith dialogue today must be about how different religious traditions see the justification (or not) of armed conflict. We have noted what the Christian Just War theory has to say about it. Is it possible for the notion of *Jihād*, for example, to be removed from extremist rhetoric so that Muslims can use it to reach agreement with Christians and others about the conditions under which armed intervention may be justified? Such agreement, or even convergence, would be of great assistance to the international community when it comes to making difficult decisions about particular cases.

Finally, Western military action in Afghanistan must be seen as being directed against radicalization of the region as a whole. We have seen its implications for Pakistan already. Since the Islamic Revolution, Iran has had its own brand of Shiʿa radicalism, which shows no signs of abating in spite of international pressure and internal dissent. China must take serious account of its own western flank and the increasing dangers of extremism in Xinjiang province. India, obviously, has an interest in making sure that it is not destabilized because of the situation in its neighbourhood. In this connection, it may be worth saying that a final settlement of the Kashmir dispute seems to be in everyone's interests: India would gain security from militant groups seeking to infiltrate not only its part of Kashmir but more widely than that. The Pakistan Army would be released from its Eastern front and be able to redeploy against extremists in the west and the north. This would also assist Afghanistan and the international forces in making sure that militants under pressure on one side of the border do not flee to the other. With the dangers of militancy removed, there is also a greater chance for a semblance at least of democracy to emerge in the new Central Asian republics. These are important gains and we must not lose sight of them.

We have argued, therefore, for a comprehensive strategy against militancy and for pacification on both sides of the Durand Line. The involvement of the international community in Afghanistan must lead to a strong civil society and the rule of law. Women should be emancipated, young girls given the opportunity for education and for freedom of belief and expression to be promoted. There should be a credible government at both the centre and in the provinces that does not tolerate corruption. In particular, there should be an effective policy against drugs that does not penalize the farmers but makes it impossible for extremists to finance themselves by means of an illicit trade in drugs.

All of this is achievable. What is required, most of all, is the will to deliver and a commitment for the medium term which will not be vulnerable to the shifting sands of popular opinion, especially at election time.

Barack Obama has decided to send in more American troops to secure crucial areas of Afghanistan, including leading cities such as Kandahar, from attack and occupation. British and some other NATO forces have also been augmented. However belated, this decision is to be welcomed and will reassure many in Afghanistan and Pakistan who have been waiting anxiously for it.

Obama is, of course, engaged in a careful balancing act. On the one hand, he has vital US interests, at home and abroad, to consider, and on the other his vociferous and influential anti-war lobby. It seems that the announcement of an 'exit' strategy at the same time as the increase in troop numbers is part of this attempt to keep everyone happy. As has been pointed out, however, this is very dangerous. It gives the *Tālibān* a date when the pressure on them will begin to decrease and they will, therefore, be able to plan for increased activity. It will further demoralize anti-*Tālibān* Afghan groups and also those in Pakistan who have been arguing for an anti-extremist policy in that country. The temptation for Pakistan and other regional powers to deal with the *Tālibān* after all will surely increase.

It should be said clearly that any increase in *Tālibān* influence and control, whether in Pakistan or Afghanistan, will not only mean that the security situation in the region deteriorates further, but it will also directly or indirectly affect Western interests. It will, once again, be possible to harbour terrorists with plans to terrorize the West and also to train those from Western countries who wish to pursue their extremist agenda in the West. Last but not least, it will mean returning significant sections of the population in the region to captivity, cruelty and barbarism.

It would have been enough to have said that the US and its allies would leave only 'when the job was done' but that they would increase efforts to hand over security matters to properly trained Afghan troops as soon as possible, without mentioning any dates, even if these are only about the beginnings of a withdrawal and even if they are conditional on the security situation as it is then. Whatever is said, and however it is said, should be such that it cannot be taken to mean a dilution of the commitment to prevent the region from being used for terrorism abroad and terrorism against the people of the region itself.

8

How to cure Pakistan of its radical Islamism

We often hear that Pakistan has lost touch with its founding beliefs. There are ways, however, of restoring that link. As children in Pakistan in the 1960s we were brought up with many Muslim friends, neighbours and relatives. At my Christian school, 90 per cent of the pupils were Muslims, but there were also Hindus, Parsis and even Pakistani Jews. From time to time there were communal and religious tensions, but these were usually resolved peacefully. Guns were hardly ever seen, except, perhaps, with security guards at banks. Such a society broadly reflected the view of its founder, Muhammad Ali Jinnah, that religion had little to do with the business of the state.

Women were free to move around and to wear what they liked. Although forbidden to Muslims, alcohol was available for those who wanted it. Karachi was a cosmopolitan city that attracted a great variety of overseas visitors. Non-Muslims could be prominent in public life and were represented in the Civil Service and the Armed Forces. There was a general spirit of give and take.

Today Pakistan has become a cockpit for radical Islamism and its terror offshoots. So, with Osama bin Laden dead, now is the time for the country to look closely at itself. What can be done?

The prominence of what has come to be called Islamism can be traced to the insecurity that Pakistan feels about its borders. Its cultivation, for example, of Afghan Islamist militants dates from before the Soviet invasion and was designed to contain Afghan ambitions in the North-West Frontier Province. Islamist militancy has also been used to further Pakistan's interests in Kashmir and, more widely, in achieving a balance of power with India. The success of Islamist groups in the north and west led to the nurturing of the 'Lashkars', militias who wished to infiltrate India-held Kashmir.

In the area, Islamist extremism has two heads; the Taliban in Afghanistan and Pakistan, and the Lashkars. Such militancy has created a 'Kalashnikov culture' and an appalling tradition of political murder, as well as a sense of insecurity for ordinary people.

Alongside these developments, the regime of the military dictator, Zia-ul-Haq, who seized power in 1977, sought legitimization by aligning itself with the religious parties. One of the features of this alliance was a programme of Islamization that included the introduction of the Shari'a, its penal law, discrimination against women, restriction on the freedom of religious minorities and the strengthening of the blasphemy laws that have now become so notorious.

For the first time, the regime began ruthlessly to propagate the Wahhabi-Salafi form of Islam. There was also a determined attempt to withdraw from the international community and to emphasize Pakistan's distinctiveness as an ideological state.

It is true that successive civilian governments have tried to halt this ideological march, but as President Zardari has said, the cancer has gone deep and is widespread.

After the murder of Salman Taseer, Governor of the Punjab, because he had advocated an amendment to the blasphemy laws, a senior government figure told me that what shocked him most was the tacit approval of the murder by a large section of the lower and middle classes. We are no longer talking about a few extremists holed up in caves in the lawless areas of the Pakistan–Afghanistan frontier but of a widespread and deeply rooted change in the mindset of many ordinary people.

If Pakistan is to hold its head high once again among the nations, a great deal has to be done – and quickly. Pakistan's friends and neighbours must do all they can to secure its borders. Both India and Pakistan should be brought to the table for a final settlement of the Kashmir dispute. This is no longer, if it ever was, a bilateral matter. Radical Islamist militancy cannot be wholly checked in Pakistan as long as Kashmir is such a central issue. With Afghanistan, much could be achieved by the international community guaranteeing that Pakistan will not be outflanked there and that its territorial integrity and legitimate interests will be safeguarded.

There is plenty to do, however, in the country itself. The media have a role to play in setting out an open and progressive vision for the nation. There should be rigorous monitoring of what is being said in the media in the name of religion and which may have the effect of promoting discrimination or violence against sections of the community. Vigilance is also needed about the teaching of hate towards people of other faiths, neighbours and the West in school and college textbooks. The tripling of British aid for education in

Pakistan is a splendid opportunity for tackling some of these issues. It cannot just be about the number of schools or pupils; there must be due attention given to what sort of education such children are receiving.

Violence against Christians and even against rival Muslim groups is often caused by inflammatory sermons from mosques and other public places. The reform of education in the madrassas, in the training of imams and in the regulation of mosques must be a top priority if there is to be communal peace in Pakistan.

I have for long argued for a programme of interfaith dialogue and research sponsored by the government of Pakistan and its friends. It would maintain a centre of excellence, organize conferences and make sure that all Pakistan's faith communities are represented at international gatherings that tackle relations between the different faiths.

There is a great opportunity at this time to have it named after Shahbaz Bhatti, the assassinated Christian government minister and activist for fundamental freedoms, with whom I had been working on such a project. Bhatti, it seemed, was assassinated because he had been named chair of a committee to review the working of the blasphemy law. It is clear that this is not acceptable to Islamist opinion.

There is a significant diaspora now of Pakistanis in Britain and in many other countries. We need to hear a clear voice from Pakistanis living abroad for an open, tolerant and progressive nation. That is what those who founded it wanted. Let us work towards it.

PART THREE

SCIENCE: EVOLUTION, BIOETHICS AND ASSISTED DYING

9

On the bi-centenary of the birth of Charles Darwin

It is a risky thing for a bishop to talk about Charles Darwin! Look what happened to 'Soapy Sam', then Bishop of Oxford.[1] I am not sure what happens to soap when it gets into hot water but nothing very pleasant, I should think.

Charles Darwin's person and work were characterized by *care*. He was industrious in his work and precise almost to a fault. He spent years in painstaking investigation of obscure botanical and zoological subjects. An example is the work he did on barnacles, for which he received a medal from the Royal Society. But he was careful also about pronouncing on things beyond his ken. He would rather say he did not know or that he was 'muddled'.

He remained *calm* in the midst of storm and controversy, and coming to Downe, in Kent, certainly helped. He was nervous and anxious in London, but Downe enabled him to look at the issues calmly and with perspective. The commitment of the Darwin family to the *community* in Downe, and particularly their continuing involvement in the church's educational and social welfare work, is a matter of gratitude for all of us.

Again and again, we find Darwin writing about the *search for truth*. He believed that there was an instinct for truth in everyone that they should follow, wherever it led. He seems never to have discussed, however, how such a noble instinct could arise from the primeval soup and among creatures struggling only to survive. Such an instinct not only leads where it will but the truth to which it leads is not just what *corresponds* to things as they are but also *coheres* with the rest of human knowledge.

In some lively correspondence with him, before and after their marriage, his wife, who was fully his equal, points out that there are other kinds of truth than simply those established by Darwin's painstaking scientific method and there are other ways to truth than such a method. Darwin himself seems to have had some experience of this, for example, when he stood in a Brazilian rainforest and was so awed by its grandeur that he wanted to cry 'Hosanna!'.

Darwin argued passionately for the *separateness or autonomy of science*. In one sense, he was wrong to do this. There can be little doubt that, as James Hannam has pointed out,[2] modern science has arisen from medieval Christian concerns to investigate a world which people believed to have been created ordered, rational and comprehensible to the human mind. In another sense, we can see what Darwin meant: scientific method cannot simply proceed on religious assumptions, it must have its independence, nor can it be beholden to foregone religious or philosophical conclusions. The process must remain open. His correspondence and discussions with friend and foe alike were characterized by *courtesy*. Even towards those with whom he disagreed the most, he was invariably courteous. It may be that scientists and theologians today can learn something from Darwin in this respect.

Randal Keynes, Darwin's great great grandson and one of his biographers, has shown how the illness and death of three of the Darwin children, but especially of their daughter Annie, greatly affected Darwin's view of *suffering* in the world and his progressive loss of faith. It is not that he was unaware of suffering before this family tragedy. He realized very well that Natural Selection and the Survival of the Fittest involved an immense amount of suffering in the world and he struggled, more and more unsuccessfully, to reconcile this with an omniscient, omnipotent and benevolent deity.[3]

Two points need immediately to be noted: Darwin *did* believe that suffering in the natural world could be justified because of the grandeur and order it produced; and he believed that suffering was justified to achieve social justice. Adrian Desmond and James Moore have shown his commitment to the abolition of slavery, even if it were at the expense of losing a million lives.[4] Given his times and his background, this assent to human equality is breathtaking and reassuring, for, as he knew, there were those who wished to misinterpret his work in the cause of what might be called 'scientific racism' and which gained currency, at different times in both Europe and the United States. From a Christian point of view, of course, the reality of suffering has to be understood in the light of a suffering God who suffers to redeem and to transform a suffering world. The theme of *sacrifice* is to be found everywhere in the living world and in human society, witnessing to its centrality for both human and natural destiny. The Cross of Jesus Christ reveals its place in God's purposes of redemption and reconciliation (Rom 8.18–25).

Natural selection is the engine, according to Darwin, that drives evolution, i.e. some heritable variations occurring in organisms can confer an advantage on them in that struggle for survival that characterizes the living world. Because they are heritable, and because organisms that have them survive, they tend to be conserved, leading to a beneficial development of the organism. The mechanism, however, for the occurrence of such variations was unknown to Darwin and became known only with the rediscovery of the work of the Austrian monk, Gregor Mendel, 18 years after Darwin's death. In short, it is spontaneous mutations in the genes of germ-line cells that cumulatively give rise to heritable variations, some of which are favourable for survival. But, as the Cambridge palaeontologist Simon Conway Morris has pointed out, not everything is possible. The course of evolution is constrained not least by its physical and environmental context. That is why, presumably, we see *convergence* in the development of organs, such as arms, legs, teeth, etc., that are similar in different species and, indeed, in like species, which are widely separated, such as the wolf of the 'Old World' and marsupial 'wolves'.

Not only do we see remarkable convergence, but also the phenomenon described as *complexification* by the great Jesuit palae-ontologist, Teilhard de Chardin. We are faced with more and more complex organisms, and now we know that this is not just at the macro level but at the micro level as well. In fact, one of the great challenges to a Darwinian view of evolution is precisely how to account for the irreducible complexity of micro-organisms such as the cell.

Although Darwin was much taken by *conflict* in nature and the struggle for survival, it is important also to note the *cooperation* that exists within and between species. The phenomenon of symbiosis has often been noted, where plants and animals cooperate to feed, camouflage and protect one another. Lynn Margulis has argued that this happens even at the micro-level and may account for the structure of cells.

Nor can we ignore the emergence of *consciousness* and its importance for survival. With humanity we reach self-consciousness and, therefore, are self-aware, questioning beings who can observe and reflect upon the universe and themselves. Does the very nature of the universe and of the evolutionary process lead up to the emergence of such beings and, if so, what is the significance of this? Teilhard thought, of course, that humans were a bridge between the natural, living world and the divine. If there are several levels of being, the material, the living, the human and the super-natural then it will be true that a higher level of being cannot simply be described in terms of the lower. Darwin sometimes gave in to this temptation and it sounds reductionist. The human search for truth, human feelings of reverence, the desire to worship, moral and spiritual values, cannot just be reduced to description in terms of animal behaviour or of physico-chemical processes.

This brings us to *significance*: whatever Darwin believed about the emergence of life on earth, it is quite clear that he believed in the significance of the universe and that it had not come into existence 'by chance'. As Christians also, we affirm not only the significance of the universe but also its purposiveness in the mind and the will of God. Not only that, we must also affirm the significance of the human person and God's purposes being worked out in us and through us. Whatever else we may deny, we cannot deny our own, immediate, sense of being agents who can act in and on the world around and make a difference, however small. We must acknowledge our power of *self-direction*, even if it is limited by our environment and our own capacities. This leads us to an affirmation of human freedom. Once again, although it is limited, it is also real. We cannot be reduced to automata and to mere physical, chemical or even biological processes. We are persons of intrinsic dignity and worth. We can act in and on our environment and we have a certain amount of freedom.

In the grand *sweep* of history it is nations and peoples with a sense of their own destiny and freedom that flourish. This may be no more than a cunning mechanism for survival, but I believe it has more to do with the impress of the divine image on us which gives us not only our dignity and freedom but also our sense of being purposive, constantly seeking to attain our own ends, personal and social, but also being aware of our journey to God and our journey in God who has brought this wonderful world into being and who sustains it at every moment of its existence.

10

Choosing life rather than death

The BBC film *Choosing to Die*, aired for the first time in 2011, has been called 'incredibly moving' and 'an affecting piece of work, in which we see a person take his own life on camera, so desperate was he to affect the debate on assisted dying'. But, of course, it is not as idyllic as it is made out to be. We know now that the dying was messy, with the dying man choking and gasping for water and the request being refused by those 'helping' him to die. The relatives, moreover, seem unconvinced and there must be serious questions about the impact on them of these deaths.

Again and again, both Parliament and the professional bodies concerned have declared their opposition to the legalization of assisted suicide. The Director of Public Prosecutions in his final guidelines has said that the presumption of prosecution will remain, whatever discretion is exercised in individual cases, and yet the issue keeps being brought back to Parliament and the public arena by a small but determined group of lobbyists. It seems that the BBC has joined this group, having broadcast five programmes on this subject since 2008, all portraying assisted suicide in a favourable light.

We must, of course, feel compassion for those who have a terminal or incurable illness and also for their relatives and friends who wish to relieve them of their suffering. The paradox is that the campaign for assisted dying has emerged at precisely the time when the Hospice movement has shown us how pain can be managed, even seriously ill patients made comfortable, and for there to be significant quality of life up to the very end. Anna, a friend of ours, has just died after four years of battling with a cancer that proved terminal. Throughout this period, she was a picture not only of dignity but of thought for others. This was also a time for her of 'putting things right' and of preparing for her passing and for what lay ahead. Her hospice helped her to manage her illness until her peaceful death.

As a priest and a bishop, I know that clergy and other carers see numerous people through terminal illness to a dignified death. Robert Runcie, the late Archbishop of Canterbury, when he was dying, was full of praise for his wonderful Macmillan nurse. Compared to the few who are willing and able to go to clinics such as Dignitas, thousands are using the hospices. My son works for a hospice that delivers care not only at their residential facility but in people's homes. It would be good if documentaries could be made about such work, and more resources, both public and voluntary, put into it. People's 'last days are not their lost days', as the founder of the Hospice movement, Dame Cicely Saunders, has said and they can continue to enjoy some quality of life, even its enrichment, and to learn more about themselves and others even at this stage in their lives.

Respect for autonomy is highly and rightly valued in the medical profession but, when a terminal or incurable condition is diagnosed, it is, rather, the close support of family, friends and the medical community that is necessary. It is relatedness and interdependence which matter. Instead of seeing themselves as alone and unwanted, people with terminal and incurable illness should be drawn into a circle of love and care where they will be valued as persons and made as comfortable as possible. One of the tragic aspects of the BBC film is the rejection of such offers of help by those who had chosen to die.

Real life is quite different from Sir Terry Pratchett's science fiction; relief from pain may, indeed, sometimes actually lengthen a lifespan but it can also shorten it. If the intention is not to kill but to alleviate suffering, even if it is thought that death might result, that is not euthanasia but falls within the sphere of legitimate care and treatment of the patient. Nor is it necessary to provide overzealous treatment or to keep alive officiously, when the treatment is burdensome and disproportionate to the relief it brings. Here both patient and doctor may accept the inevitability of death without any desire to bring it about.

Those who are arguing for assisted suicide to be legalized in this country have some very important questions to answer. If such assistance is delivered by an institution the principal purpose of which is to help someone to end their lives, do we really want such agents of death in Britain? If it is to be a relative or friend who administers the lethal dose, how can we establish intention? How can we, in a world of mixed motives, know that such a person was wholly motivated by compassion and had no other interest in the death they have brought about? What about the 'vulnerable assister' who is told, by the person wishing to die, that it is part of their duty of love and care to carry out these wishes? Most of all, in this case, there certainly is a 'slippery slope' argument. Twenty-one percent of the people who use the Dignitas 'service' do not have a terminal illness. How long will it be before those with clinical depression, a broken relationship or a bereavement are queuing up for the lethal potion?

The BBC also has some hard questions to address; its own guidelines state that the portrayal of suicide has the potential to make this appear possible, and even appropriate, to the vulnerable. The World Health Organization, similarly, warns that pictures or suicide notes should not be published and that specific details about the methods used should not be disclosed. It urges the media not to glorify or to sensationalize suicide. It is widely recognized that suicide can be imitative and that the media has to be vigilant about 'copy-cat' suicides or attempts at suicide. What evidence is there that in screening the film these serious issues were taken into consideration? Apart from legal considerations around free speech, was there any thought given, or advice sought, about the moral implications of crossing this Rubicon?

The other point, which cannot be made too strongly, is that as a public service broadcaster the BBC has an obligation to provide a balanced presentation of the moral issues of the day, especially when legality is also at stake. So far, there has been little evidence of such balance in this matter. Let us hope that even now there will be, and that discussion will not just be about the moral questions involved in assisted suicide and euthanasia but also about the responsibilities of the media in the presentation of such issues to the public.

Terry Pratchett has said, somewhat dramatically, that he would like to die sitting in his garden with a glass of brandy in one hand and life-ending chemicals in the other. His own film shows us that this soft-focus idealism is quite misplaced. He himself appears uncertain, saying he was not sure what he would do in similar circumstances and that he changes his mind every few minutes. Such an uncertain mentor is very dangerous to have in a matter of ultimate importance. Whatever he does, he seems to be talking about taking his own life, or suicide, which is not illegal in this country, rather than assisted suicide, which involves taking the life of another person and is illegal.

Is not the Judaeo-Christian tradition of the Bible a surer guide? 'Thou shalt not kill' is about acknowledging the gift and dignity of human life which, whether ours or another's, we do not have the competence to take. Much suicide and attempted suicide is born out of despair, but this teaching is about purpose and destiny for every human being, and is, therefore, about faith and hope, however desperate the circumstances. It is also about love: a proper regard and valuing of ourselves and the love which leads us to serve those in need, in this case those who are terminally and incurably ill. It is not a surprise, then, to learn of the Christian origins of the Hospice movement. Around their values a national consensus of care has developed. Let us not throw it away because of siren voices that appear not even to believe themselves what they are urging us to do.

11

The HFEA is dead

Long live a commission on bio-ethics

Many welcomed the government's decision to abolish the Human Fertilisation and Embryology Authority. It was welcomed by clinics, and by other service providers, who thought that it unnecessarily restricted their activities; and pro-life groups, which were excluded from membership of the authority and who felt that it regulated activities which should never have been undertaken, will also be delighted.

For six years, from 1997 to 2003, I served on the authority and chaired its ethics and law committee. It was a steep learning curve and there was a daily struggle to keep moral reflection up to date with scientific development and the desire of medical and commercial enterprises to use what science was making possible. In a number of areas that are morally crucial, we were able to hold the line. For example, we were able to maintain the prohibition on the production of embryos only for research. We permitted selection of embryos through pre-implantation genetic diagnosis (PGD) only when an existing child had a heritable life-threatening condition and any subsequent child was substantially at risk. I, at least, agreed reluctantly and only because the alternative could have been life-threatening both for any child to be born and for the existing sibling.

I am sorry that the HFEA became increasingly libertarian in its decisions. It ruled in favour of producing embryos purely for research through what was euphemistically called 'therapeutic cloning'. Such embryos, within a prescribed time limit, could be used to extract stem cells for research on how these cells could be used to treat a variety of diseases. It has always been a surprise to me why such high priority should be given to embryonic stem cells when, in fact, most effective treatments have been derived from adult cells which have been re-programmed to behave in a 'pluripotent' way. The HFEA not only allowed PGD to produce 'saviour siblings', even when there was no danger of life-threatening heritable disease, but, controversially, it allowed the creating of so called 'cybrid' embryos, which involve the use of an animal egg from which the nucleus has been removed and replaced with the nucleus of a human cell. It also allowed the creation of 'true' hybrids, where human sperm is mixed with animal eggs to produce 'entities'. Thankfully, at present, they have to be destroyed after 14 days, but who knows what may happen in future?

Before we celebrate its demise, however, we need to ask why the HFEA was created in the first place. It was created so that the special status of the embryo could be recognized. It was acknowledged that the embryo had all the genetic material needed for a human being and could not, therefore, be treated like any other tissue (for which there is another authority). This deliberately left open the question as to whether there was already a human being present. Even if we take a developmental view of how personhood emerges, to my mind the precautionary principle requires us to treat the embryo with respect at all stages precisely because we do not know when we are dealing with a human being.

Respect for the embryo, although in a reduced sense, was enshrined in the Act but has been steadily eroded, either because of decisions made by the HFEA or by changes in legislation. The question arises, nevertheless, as to how the special status of the embryo will continue to be recognized in law and regulated in practice.

There remain many important issues that have to do not only with the status and treatment of the embryo but with the welfare of any children born as a result of fertility treatment. Whatever we think of such treatment, the reality is that it is here now with us and it needs to be strictly regulated.

One possibility may be to create a body along the lines of the United States President's Commission on Bio-Ethics. Its remit would be wider than that of the HFEA and it would have a membership that was comprehensive and independent. For example, it could have people from pro-life groups as well as others. It could have a deliberative as well as a regulative function. One of the problems with the HFEA was that the pressure for inspections and regulations squeezed out the opportunity for serious reflection on the moral issues confronting our age. This could sometimes lead to taking the line of least resistance. If such a new commission is to be created, there should be a wide-ranging public discussion about its terms of reference, its membership, its relationship to Parliament and government and whether it will be advisory or statutory. It should not be necessary to create a vast bureaucracy to run it. A number of existing organizations of all shades of opinion as well as volunteers with expertise could assist in its operation.

Such a commission would continue to offer advice on the moral status of the embryo and on the strict limits there should be on what can be done with it. It would be concerned with the need that people have for knowing their complete genetic inheritance (this, by the way, is one reason for the importance of the biologically-related family). It would engage with the demonstrable need that children have for both parents, and how parents can play a complementary role in the upbringing of their children.

There are also serious moral issues about the storage of both eggs and embryos and how they are to be used. If embryonic stem cells become important for treatment, the emergence of banks for cord-blood will become a morally acceptable way of using such stem cells, particularly if it is to benefit the donors themselves or their near relatives. The outcomes of *in vitro* fertilization (IVF) will need continually to be monitored, as will the welfare of any children born in this way. New technology will have to be considered not only for its moral acceptability but also for its practicality and affordability. Researchers and practitioners will have to be held to account. The work of the Human Genetic Commission could also be brought within the remit of such an extended commission.

It may be that the HFEA has run its course, but the moral and social issues which brought it into being have not gone away. They are still with us – and, arguably, in a sharper form. We need a body that will not only monitor and regulate but which will be able to provide moral direction in areas which are, sometimes, quite uncharted.

I understand that the Government is considering allowing some advisory mechanisms, along the lines of the HFEA's Ethics and Law Committee, as a way of ensuring that the ethical aspects of treatment and research are given the attention they deserve. If so, this is not so far from the kind of commission I am proposing. Such a body will need to be independent and well-respected if it is to carry any clout. It must also balance the interests of the stakeholders – fertility clinics, medical practitioners and scientific researchers – with those of the general public. Apart from scientists, philosophers and theologians, it is of crucial importance that wider society should be represented on such a body. It is important that such a body is not constrained in any way, either in coming to a mind on an issue or in offering its opinion to the government, Parliament and the public. If it has advisory rather than a statutory rôle, this may enable it to sometimes offer a range of options for the consideration of those who are to make the necessary decisions.

12

Is Mary Warnock's *Dishonest to God* honest?

Mary Warnock's *Dishonest to God* is a swashbuckling and iconoclastic book: Warnock at her best or, as some may say, at her worst![1] What we have here is a strongly voiced version of the *zeitgeist* masquerading as high philosophy. It has to be taken seriously, however, for it reflects much conventional thought and underlies a great deal of contemporary policy and legislation. Her theological bias is immediately revealed when she tells us that people who have influenced her most include the radical bishop Richard Holloway, the sceptical New Testament scholar Dennis Nineham, and the deconstructionist theologian Maurice Wiles. Not only is there a hint of arrogance in her claim that we live in a more 'clear-headed' age than that of Aquinas or Duns Scotus but she shows her prejudice, again and again, by misrepresenting, for example, Roman Catholic teaching on sexual ethics, by not setting out its full range, and by using emotive language about supposed papal claims.

She admits that morality is needed for policy-making and for legis-lation but attempts to prise it apart from its religious basis. Her ground, it seems, for doing this is the claim that, because people are no longer religious, a secular basis has to be found for morality. This is rather like claiming that, because they are no longer philosophical, there is no need for philosophy, or, because they are not very scientific, there is no need for science. In fact, it is demonstrably the case that the great moral systems of the world have been developed within particular religious traditions; whether it is the Laws of Manu, The Torah, The *Shari'a* of Islam or Christianized Roman Law and The Canon Law of the Church which have so influenced the emergence of public law in the West.

Very little is said about the influence of the Bible on the notion of an ordered universe on which the predictability, verification and falsification requirements of modern science are based. Nothing is said about the debt we owe to the Bible for our view of Time as a forward, progressive and purposive movement. Nor is there any discussion as to how the intrinsic dignity of human beings is related to the biblical teaching on being made in God's image. Historically speaking, the Enlightenment acquired this language from Christian discourse regarding the natural rights of the indigenous peoples of the Americas and the various declarations, such as the United Nations Universal Declaration on Human Rights, reflect this heritage. It is noteworthy that Islamic countries have had difficulty in recon-ciling this Declaration with the provisions of *Shari'a*. Given the Judaeo-Christian origins of this discourse, other religious traditions may be able to find a basis for the affirmations of this Declaration within their own sources. Atheists and agnostics too would have to ground such a belief in human dignity in some other way. What cannot be allowed is a mere affirmation without any basis for it. The world is too full of genocide, oppression, unjust discrimination, the violation of the weak and the defenceless for such a *laissez-faire* attitude. For certain basic values, we need to invoke transcendental truths; whether it is the image of God for human dignity, a belief in the common origin and destiny of the human species for equality, or the freedom and moral agency of the human person in the context of a just and ordered society.

A Judaeo-Christian moral worldview arises not only from how the world is but what it is that makes for its *shalom* or welfare and what it is that makes for personal and social flourishing. In other words, it also arises from a vision of how the world should be. An objective basis for morality needs to take account of not only how the world is but what makes it like it is and also how humans may find meaning, purpose and direction in it. The moral realism of Warnock's colleagues, Elizabeth Anscombe and Philippa Foot, was grounded in theism; would that it were so also of her. Without it, she is exposed, on the one hand, to subjectivity, variation and endless reinterpretation. As we shall see in a moment, this has huge implications for her work in the public sphere. On the other, her religion is reduced to the aesthetic akin to, and comparable to, music. The aesthetic dimension is, undoubtedly, important for religion, but most religious people would agree that religion cannot simply be reduced to an appreciation of music.

Her willingness to abandon moral realism for a subjective and variable approach is seen most clearly in her treatment of life at its earliest and latest stages. Warnock became (almost) a household name because she chaired the Committee of Inquiry that produced

the Warnock Report of 1984 which was the basis for the Human
Fertilisation and Embryology Act (1990). Her own account of this in
the book shows that she and the Committee were far from impartial,
and that certain conclusions – for example, permitting research on
embryos – were foregone. In a knockabout argument she claims that,
because an embryo consists of only a few cells, it should be denied
any application of the concept of justice. But why should the size of
an individual determine whether they deserve justice or not? Is her
view incremental, so that a baby would deserve less than a child and
a child less than a grown-up? She seems to believe that a developmental view of the emergence of personhood implies that there is
a time when the embryo is not a person and so can be manipulated
and destroyed. But surely, even such a view suggests that we do not
know exactly when there is a human person, and this should, rather,
be an argument for applying the precautionary principle at all stages
of embryonic development. In fact, much of the hope from stem cell
research, for example, has come from the use of adult cells, which can
be reprogrammed to develop into different kinds of cells for blood,
muscle or bone, rather than from the much trumpeted embryonic
research which has produced little by way of application. Even with
'embryonic' stem cells, it may well be that obtaining them from
placental and cord material will prove more useful than from human
embryos directly.

    In her enthusiasm for embracing 'liberality', she becomes more
and more libertarian. She is willing even to countenance repro-
ductive cloning so that a couple may have a child, paying no heed
to the welfare of such a child and neglecting warnings about genera-
tional confusion and disordered relationships where a cloned child's

biological parents would be its grandparents and where the child would be a near-identical, but much younger, twin of one of its 'parents'. Has she taken account of the careful discussion, for instance, in the Report on Human Cloning of the US President's Council on Bioethics?[2]

Changes to the 1990 Act, which have been mainly for the worse, she claims have been 'fairly minor'. These include the removal of the requirement that account be taken of the need a child has for a father, the widening of permission to use embryo selection, through Pre-Implantation Genetic Diagnosis, to assist siblings even with non-heritable diseases, and the permission to create both 'cybrid' (where an enucleated animal egg is fused with a human cell) and true hybrid (where human sperm is mixed with animal eggs) embryos. Many will think that these changes are far from minor and reflect the extent to which we have lost our moral bearings.

I agree with her when she argues that judges and juries should be allowed to consider extenuating circumstances in a murder trial and that a judge, therefore, might have some discretion in the sentencing of the accused. I cannot, however, share her views on assisted dying. Although the view of human autonomy, which she describes, has its roots in the Judaeo-Christian tradition, such autonomy is not absolute. We are also beings in relationship to God and with one another and must respect the givenness of life in one another. Since ancient times, and not only in the Judaeo-Christian context, it has been the duty of doctors to preserve life and to relieve pain. Doing the latter may, in extreme circumstances, hasten death, but this should not be confused with the intention to kill. For a relative or a friend to assist in a suicide is also fraught with difficulties: how will we ever know, in a world of mixed motives, that the assistance was driven solely by compassion? Had the person assisting, or others, made the sufferer feel that life was no longer worth living? Was the sufferer well-informed about all the options, and what was his or her mental state at the time of making the decision?

At a time when palliative care is at its most developed and hardly anyone need be in unmanageable pain (thanks to the Christian-based Hospice movement), it is all the more tragic to see people arguing for euthanasia or assisted death. It is well-documented that there can be personal and institutional pressure on those seriously ill to consider ending their lives because they do not wish 'to be a burden' on anyone. It is known also that, where euthanasia and assisted suicide are allowed, as in the Netherlands, provision for palliative care deteriorates, thus increasing the likelihood of people choosing to die and establishing a vicious cycle of permitting euthanasia, reducing palliative care and increasing the numbers of people choosing to die. No compassionate society should go this way. Its aims, rather, must be to relieve pain, provide for a quality of life at all stages and not officiously to keep alive. Patients should be free, in a proper exercise of autonomy, to refuse treatment, knowing this could lead to death, but this is not the same thing as euthanasia or assisted suicide.

Like many others, Warnock was unduly optimistic about the guidelines that the Director of Public Prosecutions was asked to issue by the Law Lords at their last sitting before they were transmuted into the new Supreme Court. Aside from the question as to whether the DPP should ever have been put in this position, his guidelines, in the event, were remarkably conservative, declaring that the presumption of prosecution would remain and tightening up on the draft guidelines to a considerable extent.

Behind all of this is the notion of intrinsic human dignity that cannot be taken away by other humans, except in very clearly defined and limited circumstances such as self-defence. The question is whether Warnock recognizes it and upholds it. It is true that some theological concepts are *a priori* (such as that of intrinsic dignity), but this does not mean that *a posteriori* arguments are excluded from a consideration of how human dignity is valued in every society. Warnock seems to want to drive a wedge between these, but Christians should not agree; if God's gracious ordering of this world is violated, the consequences for individuals and societies are bound to be serious.

Warnock is right to point out the flaws in a purely utilitarian view of policy and legislation and also in Bentham's legal positivism. She agrees that, at least sometimes, there should be an appeal to a higher or moral law, but the instances she gives (the American Declaration of Independence and its descendents) owe much to thinkers like Sir William Blackstone and their appeal to Natural Law. Does she agree, then, that there is a transcendental basis for fundamental values that a mere change in public opinion or utilitarian considerations cannot alter? Apparently not, for she lapses into the language of legal positivism when arguing that Christians and others should not have matters of conscience recognized in today's so-called equality legislation.

There is a kind of naturalism in her treatment of religion; the mystery of nature and the authority of law derive from a God who reveals himself, not the other way around. She seems unaware of those who, unlike her mentors, take the historical, literary and archaeological background to the Bible with the utmost seriousness *and* uphold its once-for-all nature and moral and spiritual authority. Once again, she offers here an 'either/or' that is unnecessary. She seems to hold a 'Hindu' view of the relation between revelation and history when she declares that the question 'did it really happen?' is irrelevant. Jack the Giant-killer (her example), however suggestive, is patently a work of fiction, but the Gospels are history, albeit a special kind of history, which leads to faith and commitment. The biblical narrative is about God's presence in the world that challenges, judges, saves and transforms; it is *not* a pointing to some 'platonic' unchanging truth. Truth is personal and, therefore, dynamic rather than merely intellectual.

She writes of the 'the Spirit of Man' as the creator not only of humanity and law but of religion as well. Even if we were to agree, we would still have to ask from where has it come? Is it a surd element in an ultimately irrational universe (it is interesting to note how quickly secular rationalism leads to this) or is it a unique part of an ultimately rational, purposive and understandable universe? Why throw away the notion of a creative God because of the somewhat child-like objections of a Ruth Rendell? Is there, then, dishonesty in continuing to behave, as she does, *as if* there is a God?

Christianity has now for two millennia awakened, completed and articulated the moral sense of numerous peoples and nations. For those who will let it, it still continues to do so. Warnock's version of a mystery religion is no match for the vigour of the Christian faith. The argument for a role for religion in the public sphere need not be, indeed must not be, about theocracy. It is rather about the need for a moral and spiritual tradition on the basis of which policy decisions can be made and legislation drafted. The function of such religion would be to persuade by the quality of its arguments but not to coerce. It would be to draw attention to the basis of a nation's institutions, laws and values whilst also providing a means of critiquing what is unjust, oppressive or unnecessarily restrictive.

Mary Warnock has written a stimulating book, but she cannot have it both ways; she cannot be a moral realist who bases her morality on how things are and, at the same time, claim that fundamental moral principles derived from such a view may change over time, be given a new sense by people of imaginative genius or revolutionary spirit or, indeed, be completely rejected. Biblical and Historical Christianity, which she disavows, can at least claim some consistency in how it derives its morality from its worldview.

PART FOUR

POLITICS: VALUES AND GOOD GOVERNMENT

13

A cure for our national amnesia

It is both rare and welcome to have a speech from the Secretary of State for Education, at a party conference, which is educating and educated. Michael Gove's speech at the 2010 Conservative Party Conference in Birmingham, particularly the section on the curriculum in our schools, repays careful study. He is generally right in his emphasis on the rigorous study of traditional subjects rather than wasting time on what he calls 'pseudo-subjects'. As a student of English, we would expect him to focus on the teaching of language and literature – as he does. His choice, though, of the 'greats' could have been expanded to include Herbert, Donne, Newman, Hopkins, Eliot, Chesterton, Greene and Belloc.

It is, however, his comments about the teaching of history that are the most telling. He reminds us of that sundering of our society from its past, which I have called 'national amnesia', and asserts that, until we understand the struggles of the past, we will not be able to value our hard-won freedoms. All of this, and more, is music to my ears, but the proof of the pudding will be in the eating.

We must, of course, make sure that the teaching of history is not just about a number of significant events and personalities and that there should be a connected narrative. But how is this to be achieved and what is the 'golden chain of harmony' that can provide the connection? Surely, this has to do with a worldview that underlies the emergence of characteristically British institutions and values, such as the Constitution itself ('the Queen in Parliament under God'); a concern for the poor; a social security net, based on the parish church, which goes back to the sixteenth century; and personal liberties as enshrined in Magna Carta.[1]

The worldview that made possible the emergence of these fundamental building-blocks in our national life is, of course, the Judaeo-Christian tradition of the Bible. This is evident, for instance, in the way the Anglo-Saxon assembly, the Witan, developed, and the role of the Church in this development. Such a role has continued to be influential from the time of the Model Parliament of 1295to this day. The question now, of course, with parliamentary reform hovering in the wings, is how the Judaeo-Christian tradition can continue to be called on, especially when proposed legislation or government policy raises important moral issues for the individual and for society.

Both Edward the Confessor and the saintly Alfred made sure that English Common Law was founded on Judaeo-Christian principles, whilst respecting the customs of the people inhabiting these islands at the time. Christianized Roman Law, similarly, was studied in the universities and schools and was also mediated through the Canon Law of the Church, which dealt for centuries with matters such as marriage, family, provision for the poor and as a recourse for justice when it could not be obtained in any other way. It is only recently that public doctrine on marriage, family and the protection due to the human person, derived from the teaching of the Bible, has been set aside in favour of libertarian novelties that refuse socio-religious sanction for sexual relationships and that are able to limit the notion of personhood to accommodate scientific and commercial interests or, indeed, the particular wishes of individuals.

It was not only the area of law. Virtually every other kind of knowledge was mediated either by the Church or by Christians in their respective fields. It is often claimed that there was much knowledge in this country, until fairly recent times, of the classical literature, art and philosophy of the Greeks and the Romans. This is certainly the case but, as Pope Benedict has pointed out, this was often a knowledge 'purified' of the cruelty, promiscuity, inequality and idolatry of paganism. The encounter of Christian faith with Greek philosophy, for example, was providential, as the Pope has put it, for the intellectual history of Europe, but we must be clear that it was Jerusalem and not Athens that provided the fundamental orientation for the flowering of a Christian humanism at the time of the Renaissance and the Reformation. As Western Europe regained Hellenistic learning from the Islamic world (which had itself gained it largely from oriental Christian clergy), it also critiqued it from the point of view of Christian belief. Basic teachings, derived from Hellenism, on the eternity of the world, the denial of personal immortality and the resurrection of the dead and the primacy of philosophy over revelation were rejected because they were contrary to the Word of God.

One of the significant changes that have been noticed in the transition from the mediaeval to the modern period is the increasing emphasis on an ordered universe that has definite laws governing its workings. We can call this the 'Newtonian Paradigm', and it is responsible for the great leap forward in the theoretical and experimental study of science. The eminent Sinologist Joseph Needham, in his life-long study of the civilization of China, asked why it was that Chinese civilization, which had been so far in advance of Europe's, began to fall behind towards the end of the mediaeval and the beginning of the modern period. Very reluctantly, he came to the conclusion that it was because of the influence of the Christian view of an ordered universe, in which there was predictability, that European science advanced and the Chinese fell back. Nor is this a matter only for antiquarian interest. I am informed by generally reliable sources that China remains interested in the effect Christianity has had on Europe, not only in the area of scientific development, but also in the ordering of society and in the management of change. The Newtonian Paradigm has been under pressure, of course, not least from developments in science itself such as quantum physics but, as Professor Polkinghorne has pointed out, the world remains a cosmos whose orderly pattern we can observe and admire.[2] This last point should not be neglected: the transparency of an ordered universe to *our* mental processes is itself a matter for wonder. We should be clear that, whilst the laws of physics describe the universe as it is, they are not the cause of it. Both they and the universe demand a deeper explanation than that 'they just are'. The Judaeo-Christian tradition provides this in terms of a rational Creator who is the creator not only of an ordered universe but of rational beings, such as ourselves, within it who can, even if in a limited way, seek to understand at least something of its immensity and complexity.

Based on predictability, repetition, verification and falsification, the scientific method has been very successful, not only in identifying *what* it is that makes up the universe, but also in discovering *how* things work, as well as how they can be made to work for human advantage. Such a method, however, cannot answer the *why* questions, especially why there is something rather than nothing, or why the universe is not simply chaotic or ordered in a way not congruent with the workings of our own minds.

Similarly, to describe the process of complexification, convergence and the rise of consciousness in the course of evolution is not to explain why living matter has the capacity to make itself and why creatures evolve in these ways. Nor can such descriptions give an answer to the 'what for' type of question. What is the world for? What are *we* here for? Have we a destiny and is there ultimate purpose to our short lives? Teleology is extremely important for our understanding of ourselves and of the world in which we live. Such an understanding will surely influence how we treat the creation around us, our fellow human beings and what estimate we have of ourselves.

The biblical idea of Time as a progressive, forward movement underlies not only our sense of history, but the very possibility of development and progress. This is a quite unique gift of the Hebrews, which has largely been distributed by the Christian Church.[3] Ancient ideas of Time are usually cyclical, with endless repetition and rebirth. They would have been quite useless to an open, progressive and scientific civilization. A Christian view of Time also provided for periods when we would be taken 'out of ourselves' and become more aware of transcendence. The processes of secularization have 'flattened' Time into mere chronology. Tellingly, Holy Days have become holidays.

We have, of course, to admit that fine Christian ideals about a society based on divine justice and mutual obligation have been violated and spurned by ruthless and wicked rulers. Human dignity, based on the Bible's teaching that we have been created in God's image, has been honoured more in its breach than in its observance. There is both light and darkness in our history. Both honour and shame. We have to repent of the perfectly vicious pages of our history; whether it is the reprehensible institution of slavery or depriving indigenous people of their land and wealth, or the exploitation of men, women and children in the fields, mines or factories of this country. There are, however, also the 'perfectly virtuous pages' of our history, which have been lamentably neglected. As far back as Anselm, Archbishop of Canterbury in the eleventh century, slavery was condemned as contrary to Christ's teaching. The struggle against the slave-trade and then slavery itself, stemming from the Evangelical Revival in the eighteenth century, was explicitly Bible-based and held that we could not enslave those who shared a common humanity with us and had been created for the same freedoms as we were ourselves. It should not be forgotten that this struggle went hand-in-hand with the battle to improve the working conditions of men, women and children in the mills, mines and factories of early industrial Britain. Universal education is a creature of the churches and of Christians, not of government of any political hue. It began because literacy was regarded as vital for an informed faith and a moral life. Such an aim is worthy of education even today. The revival of nursing as a profession was, once again, the result of Christian commitment to the sick and needy. It is ironic, indeed, that nurses cannot now pray at work, under threat of dismissal, when their ward duties often began with prayer right up to the middle years of the twentieth century. So many of the precious freedoms that we value today, the fair treatment of workers and the care of those in need, arise from values given to us by the Judaeo-Christian tradition. These values, however, are grounded in the moral and spiritual vision of this tradition. It cannot, by any means, be taken for granted that they would survive for long if the tradition itself is jettisoned.

The prophetic trajectory in the Bible, confirmed by the teaching of Jesus himself, is self-critical, relentlessly pointing out the short-comings of society, of ruler and ruled, and placing before them God's demand for justice and compassion. We should take pride in our free society, where such criticism is possible, but we should also acknowledge its origins. Not only that, the tradition itself is necessary for bringing a critique to bear on contemporary cultural mores rather than simply capitulating to them.

I am glad that the Minister is setting out to remove our collective amnesia – and to enable us to see our history as a connected whole. This will need more than imaginativeness about our relationship with our neighbours or our environment. It will have to mean also the rediscovery of our spiritual and moral identity and, therefore, of that which has given it birth.

The Judaeo-Christian tradition certainly provides the connecting link to 'our island story'. Without it, it is impossible to understand the language, the literature, the art or even the science of our civilization. It provides the grand themes in art and literature, of virtue and vice, atonement and repentance, immortality and resurrection. It has inspired the best and most accessible architecture and it undergirds and safeguards our constitutional and legal tradition.

But, of course, the tradition of the Bible is wider than that. Its concern is for the whole of humanity and in a rapidly globalizing world it is becoming an important way of understanding the spiritual and moral dimensions of life without yielding to the temptation of becoming a totalitarian ideology that seeks to provide for even the minutiae of daily living and leaves little room for freedom. As Peter Hitchens has shown, atheistic secularism also leads to totalitarianism by a different route.[4] There is plenty of recent history to justify this thesis. Will we choose the renewal of a tradition that, as T. S. Eliot saw, is at the root of almost everything we value, or is it our future to wander in a sea of moral and spiritual eclecticism without a compass to give us our bearings?

14

The moral and spiritual challenge facing the Coalition

Everyone expects the Coalition government to give priority to reducing Britain's debt and to maintaining its creditworthiness. We also expect it to deal firmly with sleaze at Westminster and beyond and to restore confidence in the political process. None of these is easy to do, especially in coalition. We should be realistic, therefore, and patient.

We should, however, also be prepared to say 'it's not just the economy, stupid' nor is it just the expenses claimed by Members of Parliament. We are experiencing a deep malaise in our national life and we should be prepared to identify the causes and address them together.

What lies behind the financial crisis is massive moral failure. We have a relatively few very wealthy individuals and institutions but a whole nation massively in debt. Instead of a culture where making more and more money is the main criterion of success, we ought to be encouraging a professionalism which sees working in finance just as much a vocation as working in the caring professions. The best of British commercial practice was rooted in the Bible's vision of our responsibility for one another and for the rest of God's creation. The experiment in selfishness has not succeeded. It is time to see how a biblical view of stewardship can help us in this new and fraught situation. The political crisis, similarly, revealed weaknesses in the formation of character. We need a programme for moral and spiritual renewal so that homes and schools can, once again, be places where character can be formed.

In a situation of political division, there are bound to be disagreements about policy and even about fundamental beliefs. We should all be able, however, to agree about certain basic values although we may disagree about how they are to be promoted and where they apply. For example, whatever specific policies the government may pursue, it must be clear in affirming human dignity. This must be so for the poor abroad, but also for the weakest and most vulnerable at home, whether these are people with special needs, the homeless, the youngest or the oldest.

There is a great equality industry around, but we have to ask why we think human beings are equal, especially when *prima facie* the evidence is of inequality: rich and poor, strong and weak, geniuses and fools, etc. Racism, chauvinism, oppression and exploitation of all kinds are forever ready to use these as an excuse for furthering their own agenda. Against our worst instincts we have to affirm what the Bible and modern science both teach – that is, the common origin of all of humanity and, therefore, of the radical equality of all, no matter what appearances may suggest. This is about who people are and not necessarily about what they do or how they choose to live their lives.

There is much concern, across the political spectrum, of a steady erosion of liberty in the last several years. Once again, human freedom is a profoundly spiritual matter and has emerged from the Bible's view of the person as a responsible moral agent. We look to the new government to uphold the basic freedoms of belief, of manifesting one's belief and of expression. In the unenviable task of balancing legislation, we expect a recognition of and respect for conscience which is properly formed and which stands within a serious moral tradition.

Many of our fellow-citizens rightly expect the government to address issues of safety and security in making our streets safe and protecting us from terrorists. It is important, however, for the government to protect not only individuals from harm, but also those arrangements and values which make for a free and ordered society. This will include the protection of fundamental freedoms and of institutions like an impartial judiciary, a sovereign Parliament and strong family relationships.

There is much for government to do, but the agenda should not be, cannot be, limited to the economic and social issues confronting us, for behind them lie huge moral and spiritual questions about how human beings are to be treated.

15

Failures both economic and moral

By any standard of measurement, 2009 was a momentous year. The financial crisis had us reeling as the value of our savings and our homes plummeted. As people felt less secure about their jobs, they spent less and gave less. Not only did High Street businesses suffer but charities were also affected. It is true, of course, that the financial crisis was brought about by a failure of regulation, especially in taking account of the growing complexity of global market transactions. But it was also brought about by moral failure. Even if we grant that market processes are 'amoral' in themselves, we cannot deny that we are moral agents as we act within those processes and are thus responsible for our actions. In the past, the best of British financial and commercial life was characterized by the values of responsibility, honesty, trust and hard work. Such values arose from a specifically Christian view of accountability before God, the sacredness of even the most humble task (as George Herbert said, 'who sweeps a room, as for thy laws, makes that and the action fine') and the recognition of mutual obligation by people of all classes and callings, one towards another. This rich tradition was set aside in favour of an entrepreneurial 'free for all' and 'winner takes all' ethos. We are now seeing the results. Far from engendering the wealth which would have benefited society as a whole, it has actually left not only this generation but future ones as well in such significant debt that it will affect the lives of us all for the foreseeable future.

Just as we were staggering back to our feet, we were hit this time by the political fireball. Once again, it is important to see this as a moral, and even a spiritual, crisis. This is so in two ways: first, the weakening of a moral and spiritual framework for society has left people without an anchor for the mooring of their moral lives and without guidance by which to steer through the Scylla and Charybdis of contemporary dilemmas; second, the lack of a framework has meant that there is no touchstone by which to judge a person's actions as right or wrong. No wonder everyone has been doing what is right in their own eyes and to their own advantage. It is clear that simply tinkering with political structures and processes will not solve the problems. A smaller parliament or electoral reform may be good things to have, but they will not address the questions we are facing and have to answer. These have to do with a clear moral and spiritual framework for public life. The values of human dignity, equality, liberty and security, as well as virtues such as selflessness, sacrifice and service, have arisen from a Judaeo-Christian worldview. It cannot be assumed that they would also necessarily have arisen from other worldviews, though agreed values with people of different worldviews can, of course, be negotiated on the basis of the Judaeo-Christian tradition. Any Code of Conduct for MPs, for example, should both acknowledge and draw upon such a rich moral and spiritual tradition rather than, once again, dishing out the familiar, politically correct, but empty of content, panaceas of the past.

Simply extolling 'Britishness' or 'British values' is not enough. It is not enough even to remind ourselves of the importance of Christian faith for Britain. We need to ask, first of all, *how* our understanding of the basic political and social institutions of public life is affected by our knowledge of the ways in which Christianity has shaped them. This will shed, I believe, a flood of light on their basic purpose, on how they have developed and what shape they might take in the future. If our understanding of these institutions, their origin and purpose is superficial and functional, this will have an adverse effect on the depth of our commitment to them.

We have to go on and ask *how* a Christian vision, its values and virtues, impinges on our day to day life and the questions this raises. We have seen already how this is crucial to personal integrity in public life. So many of our moral dilemmas have to do with a proper estimate of the human person. These arise, in their sharpest forms, when persons are most vulnerable, when they cannot defend themselves and where society has the task of protecting them. In other words, they arise at the earliest stages of personhood and at the latest, when there are questions of mental capacity or even of mental illness. Without a lode-star, such as the *imago dei*, we could quickly run aground on the rocks of crude utilitarianism (the weak can be sacrificed for some greater good or the good of a larger number) or be marooned on the shifting sands of public opinion polls. For instance, whilst it may be correct to take a developmental view of the emergence of a human person through the stages of fertilization, implantation, the beginning of brain activity and so on, we still

cannot say exactly *when* there is a person. Instead of greater permissiveness, this should lead to greater caution about any procedures
that aim to manipulate the early foetus or embryo to benefit someone
else. We should also be concerned for its integrity as personhood
unfolds.

At the other end of the lifecycle, while it is never permissible to
kill, we are not officiously required to keep alive either. People may
decline medical intervention, if they are competent to do so, and
death may result when the primary aim is to relieve pain. Living wills
may also be respected, though they pose certain dilemmas of their
own. If, for instance, they are made too far in advance of the circumstances contemplated, they may not be able to specify exactly what
the person concerned is wishing to refuse or to accept. If, on the other
hand, they are made in the course of a serious illness, the question
would be whether a person's judgement is clouded by their illness
or even by direct or indirect pressure from relatives. In any event,
it cannot be permissible actively to take life, or to assist in doing so,
even in situations where a person is alive but not responsive to our
signals or to the environment generally. This is because the dignity
of personhood is inalienable and cannot be taken away by human
agency, except, perhaps, in clearly specified circumstances such as
self-defence or a just war.[1]

A widespread nihilism in culture has led to a lack of consensus
about the sacredness of the human person and, in turn, this provides a
context for the horrendous and mindless violence inflicted on people,
even on young children. We cannot expect respect for the person if
we do not give any reasons why persons should be respected. *Mutatis
mutandis*, this is also true of racism. The Judaeo-Christian tradition,

based on the Bible, teaches the common origin and equality of all human beings. It may be that Christians have not always upheld such equality in practice, but without its basis, as we have seen in doctrines of 'scientific racism' and eugenics, the weak will have no defence against oppression and exploitation by the powerful.

The family is an important aspect of biblical anthropology that sees man and woman as ordered to one another in a stable relationship of receiving and giving. It is this mutuality and complementarity that provides not only support and companionship but the stability required for the nurture of children. The family then is a basic unit of society, and any dysfunction there will surely affect other areas of our social life. It is true, of course, that Christians themselves have sometimes used family structures to abuse and exploit the more vulnerable members of the family, often women, children or the elderly. In this they are not alone, as such abuse of the family is widespread and can be seen in many parts of the world. But does such abuse or misuse justify the full frontal attack on the family that we have seen in most Western countries in the last 50 years or so? The Office for National Statistics and other bodies regularly publish figures for marriage, divorce, single-parent families, cohabitation and how long marriage lasts, etc. This is not the place to go into the detail of these figures, save to note the social devastation they represent: families everywhere with a parent (usually the father) absent, the psychological trauma of broken relationships, children without crucial bonding with one parent (usually the father), and for boys the lack of a role model as they grow up.

In fact, the attack on the family has been part of a wider aim to subvert the fundamental institutions of society because they were regarded as bourgeois, patriarchal or exclusive. At first, this was to prepare the ground for a Marxist-type political revolution. When this did not come about, the social revolution became an end in itself, the purpose of which was to free individuals from cumbersome ties so they could better fulfil themselves. Relationships should be entered into freely without social coercion, it is held, and should last only as long as they nurture an individual's self-fulfilment. If and when mutual desire ceases, it is both 'wicked and useless' to seek a continuation of the relationship which is generated by the persons themselves, as Anthony Giddens has taught, and is not about satisfying a formal socio-religious criterion (in other words, the commitment and obligations of lifelong marriage)

It is not a surprise that, with these views, a plethora of relationships in which there is due consent and which do not exploit the young or vulnerable, will increasingly be seen as valid expressions of being 'family'. Such social constructivism will either treat with amused contempt or actively oppose any attempt to uphold a normative view of the family which values permanence, stability, responsibility towards one another and towards any children or, indeed, which regards the family as a basic unit of society and thus fulfilling a vital social function.

The abolition of the family is certainly one of the causes of social dysfunction and of fragmentation in our society, but it is not the only one. An all-pervasive historical amnesia is another. People are simply not told about the foundations on which their society is built or about the positive aspects of their history. No wonder, then, that when they have to grapple with cultural and religious difference they have no vantage point from which to tackle the issues which arise in a plural society. Let it be understood right away that diversity is to be celebrated and respected and can enrich any society. A Christian view of society would have emphasized hospitality for those coming to live in this country as well as being the means of welcoming their contribution to the development of social and political discourse. At the same time, it would have continued to uphold the common good which would necessarily have included a concern for the most disenfranchised of those who were here already and also for the social and economic fabric of the nation in relation to a changing demography. What we got was a multiculturalism built on amnesia. On the grounds of tolerance, it consigned newer arrivals to ghettoes where, it was imagined, they would be happier with their own kind. The housing, education and social policies of the elite, who were themselves largely unaffected by them, reinforced the separation, fostering, as we have seen, ignorance rather than engagement, fear rather than neighbourliness and resentment rather than generosity. It has led to extremisms of different kinds to flourish because of the lack of a vision of a just, compassionate and neighbourly society based on a meta-narrative which provided the grounding for adequate social capital.

We certainly need a recovery of memory; regarding the basis of our national life, a tradition of civil liberties set in train by *Magna Carta*, the Reformation's insistence on direct access to the sources of the authority (the Scriptures) for everyone, the Counter-Reformation's missionary zeal, the Christian origins of 'natural rights' language, campaigns to abolish the slave-trade and slavery, to restrict working hours and to improve working-conditions for men, women and children, universal education, the emergence of nursing as a profession, the hospice movement and much else besides. Such a recovery of memory in our schools and other educational institutions, for instance, would not be for the sake of nostalgia or to foster national pride but to provide the basis for an engagement with contemporary issues, whether these have to do with fundamental liberties, the inclusion of the marginalized, the care of the sick, or concern for the poor whether in this country or abroad.

Such a recovery of memory will make it possible for people once again to invoke fundamental principles, what Professor Peter Hennessey has called 'the timeliness of the timeless'. It is not necessary, by the way, for such an owning of the Christian vision to require a special position for a particular church. It is quite possible to distinguish, as Martin Marty has done in the American context, between civic and ecclesial religion. Whilst the churches would remain concerned, of course, to promote a Christian vision of society, a Christian-inspired civic religious sense would be distinct from each of them, as well as related to and responsive to their view of the role of religion in the public sphere.[2]

Even, and perhaps specially, in this context, the Church's prophetic role will be needed. It will still be necessary to ask for proper discernment before policies are made or legislation passed; churches will remain in the business of forming consciences and in 'telling it like it is'. There will have to be both a clear forth-telling in terms of what is good for society and what would harm it, or people within it, and a fore-telling about the consequences of misgovernment, corruption, self-indulgence and the rest. Christian faith is not simply an endorsement of the *status quo* or even a justification of history. It must also be able to bring a powerful critique to bear on our national life.

Any vision of a Christian society is strongly challenged by what may be called 'programmatic secularism'. This has its own worldview in which there is progress but no purpose, where human dignity, equality and liberty may be affirmed but there is no underlying narrative of why they should be. It often has a libertarian focus that emphasizes individual liberty but is weak on upholding vital social institutions. Its permissiveness can endanger not only social institutions such as the family, but also, for example, the human person at the earliest, most vulnerable and latest stages of life. It can be in thrall to the latest scientific possibilities and willing to give its *imprimatur* to them, regardless sometimes of personal and social consequences.

In addition to this, and arguably more widespread, is what has been called 'procedural secularism'. This assumes that the public space is a *tabula rasa* and that consensus about the issues of the day will develop as all sides contribute to the debate. In its best forms, it is willing to allow religious perspectives to be active in this debate. The problem is, of course, that the public space is not, and never has been, a blank slate on which anything can be written. It has its own plausibility structures, assumptions and norms. If these are not informed by a Christian vision, they will undoubtedly be informed by some other paradigm, whether that is Marxism, Programmatic Secularism or some other worldview. The people of this country have to decide which they would rather have: the tried and tested paradigm of the Christian faith, which, even if imperfectly understood and applied, has served them well; or untested theories which may appear to confer greater liberty on individuals but which can lead to social disaster.

The crises have revealed the peril in which we find ourselves.

What is the way out of danger? We should not put too much hope in the institutions somehow renewing themselves. What we need are genuinely popular movements for the renewal of national life as a whole. One of the elements missing in the political life of this country is Christian Democracy. I am not saying that we should simply imitate what happens in Europe and elsewhere, but politicians of all kinds should consider whether political movements founded on Christian principles would be beneficial for the political process. A 2011 gathering in London sought to bring together people from a broad and I hope wide spectrum to discuss first this issue. This was only a short but an encouraging one.

It may be that we need a grand assembly of political and community leaders and the Third Sector, as well as representatives of churches and faith communities, to discuss these issues openly and thoroughly so that a national consensus may emerge. We want a nation at ease with itself where relationships, each in their own way, are deep and enduring, where there is opportunity for the nurture of the soul as well as of the body, and where there is a clear moral and spiritual vision which is about the destiny of persons as well as communities. If we can obtain a consensus that is not only political and economic but also spiritual and moral, then these crises that we face will have been worth it.

16

What would Jesus do? Certainly not vote for the BNP

Hard on the heels of the financial crisis, we have had a political one. People were just coming to terms with betrayal by one trusted group – the bankers, custodians of our hard-earned savings. Now it has been revealed that politicians, too, have been cynically manipulating the system to gain maximum financial advantage: an advantage denied to others because of legislation enacted by the very people who were flouting it. The Press and the Police too, instead of being 'guardians' of our civil liberties, have been found morally compromised.

Understandably, the stories have caused fluttering in the dovecotes of Westminster, the City and Fleet Street. Not a day goes by without nostrums being prescribed by political leaders, social commentators and religious leaders. Some seem to believe that, simply by fiddling with processes and structures, the problem will be solved; if only we could reform Parliament, have a different electoral system or extend electoral processes to areas like policing, we would not again have to face this lack of confidence in our democratic institutions.

Others predict that a political vacuum will develop, which various kinds of extremists and mavericks will attempt to fill – even those such as the British National Party who enlist Jesus in support of their campaign, when their ideals are as anti-Christian as they come.

Yes, we need to have confidence in our democratic institutions. But this will not be engendered by tinkering. What is needed is moral and spiritual renewal. We should begin to acknowledge that a culture built on the expectation of endless growth – regardless of its effects on the environment, the person and family relationships – is not the way. Nor will panaceas based on crude utilitarianism, and an ethics based on the findings of focus groups, serve us well. We need a robust moral framework for our life together. In this country, the Judaeo-Christian tradition has provided the basis for the institutions of state, the laws of the land and the values by which we live. It has also given rise to a sense of mutual obligation which has characterized British society at its best. The notion of the human person, as made in God's image, has given us an understanding of moral agency, the formation of conscience and of freedom. Our commitment to equality derives from belief in the common origin of all human beings; our commitment to liberty from the teaching that people are created free and subject, ultimately, to God alone.

This tradition holds that creatures have been endowed with inalienable rights. Recognition of this would go a long way towards limiting the role of the state in people's lives and, by trimming the role of government, prevent the emergence of elected oligarchies, such as the ones on display at the moment. When we talk of a society built on Christian values, it is often misunderstood as a reference to intolerance, a society of exclusivity. The ultimate expression of this tendency comes in a campaign billboard, unveiled in March, which quoted scripture out of context, then posed the question: 'What would Jesus do?' The answer given was simple: 'Vote BNP'.

This was a clear example of using Christian-sounding words to promote a profoundly anti-Christian agenda. No one should be taken in by it. The policies advocated by the BNP are contrary to our belief that all human beings, regardless of race or colour, have a common origin and are made in God's image. It is this belief that underlies British values of human dignity and equality. There can be no compromise about such values. It is recognized that the number of people coming to live and work in Britain must be limited to what our social and economic fabric can sustain. Nevertheless, the Christian value of hospitality demands that those who come legally are welcomed. Providing refuge for the genuinely persecuted is also a longstanding British tradition, and must be upheld.

So when we ask 'What would Jesus actually do?', the answer is clear. He would include all in the embrace of his Father's love, and so change them that they begin to live for others, to meet the needs of strangers and to work for a just and compassionate society.

Such work is badly needed. Not only have we witnessed the sometimes deliberate destruction of a moral framework for our social and economic life in Britain, but we have also seen the steady erosion in the formation of character. For example, if the newspapers revealed anything fundamental about our political masters, it is the woeful lack of that character building which leads us to behave with integrity and put service to the nation before self. But before we give in to scapegoating people, we have to admit that there has been a lack of emphasis on the formation of conscience and moral awareness in the nation. Once, responsibility, trust, truth-telling and hard work characterized what was best about us. These are virtues derived from Christian beliefs. Have our schools and universities been inculcating such virtues? If they have, how have we come to such a pretty pass in our national life?

One of the problems with the multiculturalism that has been foisted on us by a secularist elite is that it seeks to promote an empty 'tolerance'. This leads to isolated communities which grow further apart and which can fall victim to mutual hostility. Extremists of all sorts can exploit such isolation.

A Christian moral and spiritual framework would lead, instead, to genuine hospitality towards those arriving to share our freedoms, on the basis of a principled integration into national life. Such integration would be based on sharing a common moral framework and a *lingua franca*. Integration of this kind should not be mistaken for assimilation. It is quite possible to respect people's faith, culture and language while insisting on a common framework for public life and reasoning. What should not have been done was to have pretended that the people of Britain had no vantage point, no moral or spiritual tradition, from which they could engage with newer arrivals.

In terms of our political culture, I hope that the various crises in our national life lead not to voyeurism or recrimination, but to a national catharsis, a purging of all that is unworthy. We should reaffirm a Christian basis for society and the need for a common framework for our life together. If we are looking for moral and spiritual renewal, this will mean that new people, and new kinds of people, will appear in political life. This is, of course, to be welcomed

– as long as it is understood that their participation, and ours, is on the basis of a common moral understanding. Such a transformation would do as much to restore confidence in the nation as any amount of structural or electoral reform.

17

The proof of the pudding

How churches can respond to David Cameron's speech on Christianity

By any standards, 2012 will be a very tough year for the Prime Minister: the economic crisis will continue and ordinary people will increasingly feel the weight of it. Whilst educational reforms will bring many changes, they will be resisted by vested interests. Marriage and family life are crying out for much-needed support, but will it be provided? Moral renewal in the business world is urgent. A sense of vocation, responsibility and trust should be restored but, again, there will be those who have prospered with a 'greed is good' philosophy and who do not wish to see any change.

On both domestic and international fronts, the Government faces the challenge of affirming democracy as well as the rule of law, whilst respecting freedom of expression and conscience. To what extent is it right for politicians to bring moral and spiritual consideration to the task of policy-making and of legislation, and what resources do they have in doing so?

In his landmark speech on the place of the Bible and Christianity in our national life, the Prime Minister not only noted the crucial role of the Bible in the development of English as a language and in areas such as art and literature, he also pointed out its importance for the morals and values which have made Britain what it is *and their continuing significance today*. This is very welcome, but the question that is being asked is whether and how this is to bear on policy-making and legislation in the weeks and months to come?

He showed also how the political development of the nation is inextricably bound up with Christian ideas and values. According to him, constitutional monarchy, adult franchise, the rule of law and the equality of all before the law, have clear biblical foundations. He challenged the Church, and specifically the Church of England, to provide moral and spiritual leadership for the nation. Again, such a challenge is long overdue, but it needs to be pointed out that the role of the Judaeo-Christian tradition in national life is much more important than the status and role of any particular church. Whether or not this or that church provides what the PM is asking for, the tradition must remain central to our public life.

In raising all of these issues, David Cameron has gone further than most political leaders in recent years. Much of what he has said is music to my ears and echoes many of the concerns I have had and have written about.

The proof of the pudding is, however, in the eating, and there are a number of challenges which will confront the PM if he tries to give effect in policy and legislation to some of the things he has said in this speech. One issue is that of religious literacy in the Civil Service, Parliament and local authorities. What Cameron has said about the ways in which Christian ideas are embedded in our constitutional arrangements is simply not understood any more in the corridors of power. A disconnected view of history and the fog of multiculturalism have all-but erased such memory from official consciousness. A concerted programme is needed if this literacy is to be recovered and used. Theologians, such as Philip Blond, and church leaders can help with remedial action but, in the end, this has to do with the place of the Bible and Christianity in the schools. Nor is this only about school assembly and Religious Education (important as they are) but also, for example, with the teaching of history. Michael Gove has rightly seen that history cannot be just about discrete dates and famous personalities but must be a narrative of the emergence of a people and a nation from the mists of time. For such a project, the place of Christianity is absolutely central. For better or for worse, there would not be a narrative worth the name without taking the influence of Christianity into account. As Cameron has pointed out, values-related education on citizenship, for instance, cannot ignore the fact that many of the values we hold dear, such as responsibility, honesty, trust, compassion, a sense of service, humility and self-sacrifice, have demonstrably biblical roots.

I believe that the proper relation of Religion to Science is also vitally important, and young people should be enabled to appreciate *both* the experimental methods of Science *and* the ultimate values of significance, freedom and destiny which Religion has to offer. Such a conversation must take place in the classroom if we are not to continue being divided by 'scientistic' and religious fundamentalists.

In his speech the Prime Minister reminded us that inalienable human dignity is founded on the biblical idea that we are made in the image of God. So far so good, but to what or to whom does this extend? How far back in the story of an individual is this dignity to be respected, and are there ever any circumstances when a person might lose such dignity? It was for reasons such as these that the Human Fertilisation and Embryology Act recognized the special nature of the human embryo (where all the genetic material needed for personhood is found) and established an Authority to regulate any scientific or therapeutic work that involved a human embryo. I fully support the Coalition's desire to deal with the proliferation of quangos, and the HFEA itself is not perfect by any means. In a fast-changing world, nevertheless, we need an appropriate body that can consider the moral and social implications of developments in bioethics as a whole, and advise the Government accordingly. The Government does not have to accept such advice but not to have it seems to me foolhardy. The Judaeo-Christian tradition will have to play a significant part in any such reflections on bioethical issues. Ex-President Bush's Commission on Bioethics provides one model of how this can be done in an inclusive and non-coercive way, but there are other models available also.

Again, as Cameron reminded us, the value of equality comes from the biblical teaching (now confirmed by science) of the common origin of all human beings whatever their race, colour or ethnicity. It is important to point out that this has to do with the equality of *persons* and not necessarily with the equal value of all behaviours or relationships. The equality of all before the law is an important development from Judaeo-Christian influence on the law, but so is respect for conscience, especially as it is formed by a moral and spiritual tradition such as Christianity. I would hope that legislation initiated by this Government will, more and more, respect the consciences of believers. Legislation in the United States, arising from the First Amendment to the Constitution, provides for the 'reasonable accommodation' of religious belief at the workplace, if such accommodation does not unduly burden other employees or affects the very viability of the employer's business. It is easy to see that if such a doctrine had been in place in this country we would not have seen the absurd dismissals (and even more absurd judicial decisions that upheld them) of Christians and others because they could not undertake certain tasks on account of their faith. Britain has had a long and honourable history of respect for conscience, whether in times of war or in the practice of medicine (where health workers have long been able to opt out of any procedures towards the termination of a pregnancy). The idea of reasonable accommodation could certainly provide further grounds for respecting conscience in matters that are controversial. In a positive meeting with Dominic Grieve, the Attorney General, I was able to discuss 'reasonable accommodation' with him and look forward to the idea being reflected in Government policy.

The Prime Minister is aware of the vast scale of social service, prison work, development assistance, relief of poverty and the like which churches and their agencies undertake. He is right in expecting their help with the renewal of the big society and his vision of active citizens, involved in their community and working for the common good. Churches and Christian agencies will certainly welcome greater participation in the building up of communities, but at the same time their integrity must also be respected. They cannot simply be surrogate service-providers for the Government. What they say and do springs from their beliefs, and the authorities will have to respect these, if there is to be genuine dialogue and collaboration. Let us hope and pray that the Prime Minister's recognition of the importance of the Bible and of Christianity in public life will provide a springboard for such cooperation and understanding in the days and months to come.

18

Where do we go from here?

Some concluding remarks

In what you have just read there has been an account of how Britain and its people have been formed by the Judaeo-Christian tradition of the Bible. To be sure, they have not only used this tradition, they have sometimes abused it by invoking it to justify tyranny in the nation, oppression in the family or adventure abroad. At times, they have modified the tradition, justifiably or unjustifiably, in the heat of particular historical conditions. They have struggled with it, criticized it and reviewed it, but they have always related to it.

We have also seen, however, that there are real threats to this relationship, and powerful forces which have encouraged Britain to break radically with its past, at least in this respect. The results of this fracture are there for all to see: a much-weakened national fabric, undue reliance on opinion polls and focus groups to make crucial decisions because there is no moral tradition to call upon, increasing vulnerability of those least able to defend themselves at the earliest and latest stages of life, for example, or when mental capacity has been severely reduced through illness or trauma, the dismemberment of the family and the marginalizing of fathers, leading to rootless youth without proper role models for the ordering of their lives. The list is long and intimidating.

So what can be done about it? Is a retrieval and renewal of our relationship with the teaching of the Bible possible, given the wholesale retrenchment and alienation there has been? If it is to be possible, teaching and learning are the key. Generations now have simply not been taught what we owe the Bible in terms not just of language, literature, art and architecture but the moral and spiritual fibre of a nation. I have welcomed Michael Gove's initiatives in, for example, the teaching of history. It is obvious that this cannot be simply a jumble of disconnected dates and people but must be a connected narrative of the emergence of a great nation. In this narrative, Christian faith, the Church and Christian thought must play a central part, if the story is to be at all intelligible. For instance, how the system of public law developed out of Christianized Roman Law and the Canon Law of the Church is worth knowing if people are to appreciate the moral underpinnings of our legal system.[1] The Venerable Bede is regarded as the 'Father of English History', and without his *Ecclesiastical History of the English People* it would be impossible to know very much about the early history of these islands. Theodore of Tarsus, the only Asian to have been Archbishop of Canterbury, ably assisted by Hadrian the African, set about not only demarcating the parish system, the basis of local organization, but also extending education throughout the land.[2] Immigration and diversity there have always been, but we need to learn again how to relate these to a common life and common goals.

School pupils need to be aware how the foundations of modern science were laid by Christian thinkers in the Middle Ages, and not only that, but in RE classes to seek a better understanding of the history of the relationship between Science and Religion and to take scientific knowledge seriously but not to abandon fundamental biblical insights about purpose, freedom, agency and redemption.[3] Catherine Glass and David Abbott have told the story of how, in Common Law, the Coronation Oath, the emergence of a constitutional monarchy, the resistance to slavery, and the liberties enshrined in Magna Carta, the Christian tradition played a central and unforgettable part.[4]

Not only do we have to learn about our past, we need also to use its resources today. Many of the motivations for selfless service in the local community arise from the Christian faith. The empowering of faith communities that are at the source of such motivations in individuals is obviously good for localities and for the nation as a whole. The biblical basis for integrity and responsibility in business needs to be brought out more clearly; greed is not good but is worship of what is made rather than worship of the maker. In the end, integrity and responsibility have to do with a sense of an ultimate judgement, of being held to account by what cannot immediately be seen and which is greater than ourselves. Whatever the nature of the market and its processes, we are never excused from being moral agents there as anywhere else.[5] Whilst regulation may be part of the answer to the global financial situation (remember the time when we were being told that *de*regulation was the answer?), nothing can take the place of trust, fair dealing, keeping our word, a sense of accountability and, most of all, a vocation to being in business. These are spiritual and moral dimensions of human activity and should be recognized as such.

Although radical secularists often invoke the values of inalienable dignity, equality and freedom, it is difficult for them to give an account of them, save, perhaps, to say that they just are ultimate values. On the other hand, it can be shown that these values have Judaeo-Christian origins and complete sense cannot be made of them without reference to this tradition. It is vital that the connection with the tradition should be made not only in public discussion but in the justification of legislation which seeks to protect the person, to promote the equal treatment of persons (not necessarily of behaviour) and which seeks to safeguard fundamental freedoms such as those of belief, expression, manifestation of belief, change of belief, etc. Vague references are sometimes made in Parliament and the Press, but these are not enough, for we have seen how these values can be eroded, misunderstood and misapplied when they are divorced from their grounding in a proper biblical anthropology. A judicious use of 'middle axioms', which acknowledges their debt to biblical principles, however, may be helpful in terms of developing public policy. Our ultimate view of marriage, as the one-flesh union of a man and a woman, for instance, is, no doubt, derived from the Genesis accounts in the Bible, but marriage can also be promoted in terms of legislation and public policy because of the benefits it can be seen to confer on the partners themselves, any children they have and on wider society. How this is developed in terms of fiscal and social policy will, of course, depend on circumstances, including the financial resources available to government.

There are now many organizations that seek to raise awareness and to campaign on issues, basing themselves on a biblical vision of wholeness for humanity and the created order. Thus, an agency like Traidcraft will try to show how fair-dealing with producers of basic commodities is required by biblical ideas of justice. Christian Aid and Tear Fund will also promote justice in our dealings with the poor but, especially in the emergency aspect of their work, they will call for compassion as well. Organizations like CARE (Christian Action, Research and Education) will argue for a biblical view of the family in the public forum, whilst Christian Concern will campaign on the basis of bearing public witness to Christian faith and in supporting those who have suffered because of their witness at their place of work or in their dealings with local authorities, the judiciary or government departments. The Christian Institute and the Linacre Centre engage in research on issues important for Christians. Such research is vital for Christian legislators and others engaged in public debate.

All of this is very desirable – indeed, indispensable – but it cannot replace the courage and information which Christians in public life need in order to influence public opinion and to turn the tide on the spate of national and local legislation, orders and rules which either compromise the Judaeo-Christian legacy of the nation, turn a blind eye to it or explicitly deny its relevance. This is not a time to wait and see but a time to act in an informed, prudent and committed way.

On the continent of Europe and elsewhere, especially since World War Two, Christian democracy has sometimes fulfilled the role of turning Christian principles into middle axioms which can then be used in the development of public policy. It is not necessary that such a movement be party-political in the way it has sometimes become. There is, however, a crying need for something like this to emerge within existing political parties in this country, and even, perhaps, outside them, especially if there is no room for such a movement within the existing political establishment. The recently held conference 'Beyond Individualism' gives some hope that the matter is, at last, on the agenda and that significant political theorists and actors are taking some note of it. From a Christian point of view, bringing the Bible to bear on urgent contemporary issues cannot be left to the chance that the conscience of this or that Christian legislator will lead him or her to intervene in this or that debate. We need to be more focused, pro-active and prepared than that.

It is my prayer and my hope that what is to be found within the covers of this little volume will inform, encourage and challenge Christian participation in our national life. I pray that Christians will promote truth and peace, that they will oppose what is corrupt and wrong, that they will seek renewal and reform and that they will strengthen what is right for the building up of our life together.

+Michael Nazir-Ali

January 2012

NOTES

The point of it all

1 On this see Peter Hitchens, *The Rage Against God*, London, Continuum, 2010.

2 See further T. Modood, *Multiculturalism: A Civic Idea?*, London, Polity Press, 2007; Jonathan Chaplin, *Talking God: The Legitimacy of Religious Public Reasoning*, London, Theos, 2008; and Rowan Williams, *Secularism, Faith and Freedom*, Rome, Pontifical Academy of Social Sciences, 2006.

3 Jonathan Chaplin, *Multiculturalism: A Christian Retrieval*, London, Theos, 2011. See further, David Nicholls and Rowan Williams, *Politics and Theological Identity*, London, Jubilee Group, 1984.

4 The Cantle Report – *Community Cohesion: A Report of the Independent Review Team*, London, The Home Office, 2001. See online at http://www. cohesioninstitute.org.uk/Resources/AboutCommunityCohesion (accessed 8 February 2012).

5 Chaplin, *Multiculturalism*, pp 22 and 37.

6 Jonathan Sacks, 'Has Europe lost its soul to the markets?' *The Times*, 12 December 2011, p. 18.

7 M. M. Thomas, *The Acknowledged Christ of the Indian Renaissance*, London, SCM, 1969.

Chapter 1

1 See further Maurice Cowling, *Religion and Public Doctrine in Modern England*, vol I CUP, 2003, pp 401ff and Joan Lockwood O' Donovan, *The Concept of Rights in Christian Discourse* in Michael Cromartie ed., *A Preserving Grace*: Protestants, Catholics and Natural Law, Eerdmans, Grand Rapids, 1997, pp 143ff.

2 See especially, Roger Ruston, *Theologians, Humanists and Natural Rights* in Mark Hill ed., *Religious Liberty and Human Rights*, University of Wales Press, Cardiff, 2002, pp 14ff.

3 David Bebbington, *Evangelicalism in Modern Britain*: A History from the 1730s to the 1980s, Unwin Hyman, London, 1989 pp 50ff.

4 On all of this see Charles Taylor, *A Secular Age*, Harvard University Press, Cambridge, 2007, Owen Chadwick *The Secularisation of the European Mind in the 19th Century*, CUP, 1975, Callum Brown, *The Death of Christian Britain*, Routledge, London, 2001 and Peter Mullen, *A Partial Vision*: English Christianity and the Great Betrayal, WatchHouse, London, 2010 and in *The Nation that Forgot God*, Edward Leigh and Alex Haydon (eds), Social Affairs Unit, London 2003, Ch 3.

5 eg. The *US Declaration of Independence* (1776), the *UN Declaration of Human Rights* (1948) and *the European Convention for the Protection of Human Rights and Fundamental Freedoms* (1950).

6 John Harris, *One Blood*: 200 years of Aboriginal Encounter with Christianity, Albatross, NSW 1990.

7 See Mary Warnock's *Dishonest to God*: on keeping religion out of politics, Continuum, London, 2010, pp 10, 61, 85ff.

Chapter 3

1 B. Almond, *The Fragmenting Family*, Oxford, Clarendon, 2006, pp 15f; and R. Berthoud and J. Gershuny (eds), *Seven Years in the Lives of British Families*, Bristol, Policy Press, 2000.

2 Almond, *ibid.*, pp 142f.

3 M. Nazir-Ali, *Breaking Faith with Britain*, Standpoint, June 2008, I, pp 45f.

4 A. Giddens, *The Transformation of Intimacy*, Cambridge, Polity Press, 1992.

5 R. Williams, *The Body's Grace* (2nd edn), LGCM, London, 2002, pp 6f; for a forceful critique see Jenny Taylor, *A Wild Constraint: the case for chastity*, London, Continuum, 2008, pp 102f.

6 Patricia Morgan, *Children as Trophies*, Newcastle, The Christian Institute, 2002, pp 27f.

7 Peter Richards, *The Family Way*, and Pauline Hunt, *Family Values*, in CAM

(Cambridge Alumni Magazine), 29, 2000, pp 19ff; and Martin Thompson, *Imaging Ourselves*, CAM, 50, 2007, pp 18ff.

8   A. Dean Byrd, *Gender Complementarity and Child Rearing: Where Traditions and Science Agree*, Journal of Law and Family Studies, University of Utah, Vol. 6, No. 2, 2005; J. M. Herzog, *Father-Hunger: Explorations with Adults and Children*, Analytic Press, Hillsdale, NJ, 2001; and Ross Parke, *Fatherhood*, Harvard, Cambridge, MA, 1996.

9   Rebecca O'Neill, *The Fatherless Family*, London, CIVITAS, 2002.

10   J. H. Newman, *Apologia Pro VitaSua*, London, Collins, 1959, p. 278.

11   E. G. Parrinder, *An Introduction to Asian Religions*, London, SPCK, 1958, p. 58; and Anthony Copley, *Religion in Conflict: Ideology, Cultural Contact and Conversion in late Colonial India*, Delhi, OUP, 1997, pp 184f.

12   See further *The Search for Faith*, MTAG, London, CHP, 1996, pp 74ff.

13   On secularization see Owen Chadwick, *The Secularisation of the European Mind in the* 19th *Century*, Cambridge, CUP, 1975; on the 'sudden' loss of Christian discourse in public life see Callum Brown, *The Death of Christian Britain*, London, Routledge, 2001.

14   Richard Dawkins, *The Blind Watchmaker*, New York, Norton, 1986; *The Selfish Gene*, Oxford, OUP, 1989; and *The God Delusion*, London, Bantam, 2006.

15   Alister McGrath and Joanna C. McGrath, *The Dawkins Delusion?*, London, SPCK, 2007, pp 40ff.

16   Simon Conway Morris, *The Crucible of Creation*, Oxford, OUP, 1998, pp 13ff.

17   On Teilhard's thought see R. C. Zaehner, *Evolution in Religion: A study in Sri Aurobindo and Pierre Teilhard de Chardin*, Oxford, OUP, 1971; and *Dialectical Christianity and Christian Materialism*, Oxford, OUP, 1971. For the idea of 'irreducible complexity' see Michael Behe, *Darwin's Black Box: The Biochemical Challenge to Evolution*, New York, Simon and Schuster, 1998.

18   See further C. Mann, *Lynn Margulis: Science's Unruly Earth Mother*, Science, 252: 378–81.

19   In The *Observer*, 22 February 2009, p. 31.

20   Randal Keynes, *Darwin, His Daughter and Human Evolution*, New York, Riverhead, 2001, pp 59ff.

21   See further Geoffrey Wainwright, *Lesslie Newbigin: A Theological Life*, New York, OUP, 2000, pp 256f.

22 *The Concept of Rights in Christian Discourse*, in Michael Cromartie ed., *A Preserving Grace: Protestants, Catholics and Natural Law*, Grand Rapids, Eerdmans, 1997, pp 143ff.

23 On all of this see further Maurice Cowling, *Religion and Public Doctrine in Modern England*, Cambridge, CUP, 2003, Vol. I, pp 390ff; and John Witte and Frank Alexander (eds), *Christianity and Law: An Introduction*, Cambridge, CUP, 2008.

24 See Mark Hill ed., *Religious Liberty and Human Rights*, Cardiff, University of Wales Press, 2002, pp 3f; and Roger Ruston, *Theologians, Humanists and Natural Rights*, chapter 2.

25 E. A. Judge, *Cultural Conformity and Innovation in Paul: Some clues from Contemporary Documents*, Tyndale Bulletin, No. 35, 1984, pp 3ff.

26 See further M. Nazir-Ali, *The Unique and Universal Christ: Jesus in a Plural World*, Milton Keynes, Paternoster, 2008, pp 1ff.

27 Nazir-Ali, *Breaking Faith with Britain*, p. 47.

28 See further M. Nazir-Ali, *Mission and Dialogue: Proclaiming the Gospel afresh in every age*, London, SPCK, 1995, pp 31ff.

29 See Alasdair MacIntyre, *After Virtue: A study in moral theory*, London, Duckworth, 2000, p. 263.

30 Susan Billington Harper, *In the Shadow of the Mahatma: Bishop V S Azariah and the travails of Christianity in British India*, Richmond, Curzon, 2000, p. 209.

31 See further *Embassy, Hospitality and Dialogue: Christians and People of Other Faiths* in The Official Report of the Lambeth Conference 1998, Harrisburg, Penn., Morehouse, 1999, pp 305ff. See also M. Nazir-Ali, *Citizens and Exiles: Christian faith in a Plural World*, London, SPCK, 1998, pp 115ff.

32 *The Vocation of Anglicanism*, Anvil, Vol. 6, No. 2, 1989, pp 127ff.

33 Charles H. Kraft, *Christianity in Culture: A study in Biblical theologizing in cross-cultural perspective*, Maryknoll, New York, Orbis, 1979, pp 169f, 345f.

34 See Ephraim Radner and Philip Turner, *The Fate of Communion: The Agony of Anglicanism and the Future of the Global Church*, Grand Rapids, Eerdmans, 2000, pp 2ff.

35 On the nature of dialogue see Pope Benedict XVI's Regensburg Address, *Faith, Reason and the University*, Vatican Library, 2006, and his lecture as Cardinal Ratzinger to the Presidents of the Asian Bishops' Conference, *Christ, Faith and the Challenge of Cultures*, Origins, CNS, Vol. 24:41, 30

March 1995. See also M. Nazir-Ali, *Citizens and Exiles*, pp 132ff; *Mission and Dialogue: Proclaiming the Gospel afresh in every age*, pp 75ff.

36 On this see the *Willowbank Report – Gospel and Culture*, Wheaton, Lousanne Committee, 1978.

37 On the early Church's involvement in showing compassion see Peter C. Phan, *Social Thought: Message of the Fathers of the Church*, Wilmington, Delaware, Michael Glazier, 1984, pp 20ff; and Francis X. Murphy, *The Christian Way of Life*, Wilmington, Delaware, Michael Glazier, 1986, pp 20ff.

Chapter 5

1 See Michael Nazir-Ali, *Islam: A Christian's Perspective*, Exeter, Paternoster, and Philadelphia, Westminster, 1983, pp 48ff.

2 Wael B. Hallaq, *Authority, Continuity and Change in Islamic Law*, Cambridge, CUP, 2001, pp 86ff.

3 M. Iqbal, *The Reconstruction of Religious Thought in Islam*, Lahore, Ashraf, 1971, pp 176f.

4 See further Mashood Baderin, *International Human Rights and Islamic Law*, Oxford, OUP, 2003; and Michael Nazir-Ali, *Conviction and Conflict: Islam, Christianity and World Order*, London and New York, Continuum, 2006, pp 146f.

5 Nazir-Ali, *Islam: A Christian's Perspective*, pp 105f.

6 Hallaq, *Authority, Continuity and Change in Islamic Law*, pp 62f.

7 Fazlur Rahman, *Revival and Reform in Islam*, E Moosa, ed., Oxford, One World, pp 132f.

8 Iqbal, *The Reconstruction of Religious Thought in Islam*, 192f. See also Anne Marie Schimmel, *Gabriel's Wing: A Study into the Religious Ideas of Sir Muhammad Iqbal*, Lahore, Iqbal Academy, 1989, pp 7f.

9 Iqbal, *The Reconstruction of Religious Thought in Islam*, pp 171f.

10 Iqbal, *The Reconstruction of Religious Thought in Islam*, pp 157f, 173f.

11 Colin Chapman, *Islam and the West: Conflict, Co-existence or Conversion?*, Carlisle, Paternoster, 1998, p. 125.

12 Iqbal, *The Reconstruction of Religious Thought in Islam*, pp 168f; Lucy Carroll and Harsh Kapoor (eds), *Talāq-i-Tafwīd: The Muslim Woman's Contractual*

Access to Divorce, Women Living Under Muslim Law, Grabels and Lahore, 1996.

13 Khalid Masud, *Hudood Ordinance 1979: An Interim Brief Report*, CII, 2005, pp 75.

14 H. A. R. Gibbs and J. H. Kramers, *Shorter Encyclopaedia of Islam*, Leiden, E. J. Brill, 1974, pp 413f.

15 Abul A'la Maudūdī, *Rights of Non-Muslims in an Islamic State*, Lahore, 1961.

16 Nazir-Ali, *Islam: A Christian's Perspective*, pp 127f.

17 Chapman, *Islam and the West*, pp 142f.

18 On the debate regarding the relative importance of the *ahad gharīb* see Yusuf Al-Qaradāwī on the website: Islam Online, 13 April 2006: *Apostasy, Major and Minor;* and Mirza Tahir Ahmad, *Murder in the Name of Allah*, Cambridge, Lutterworth, 1989, pp 74ff.

19 Zakī Badawī, *Freedom of Religion in Islam*, paper to a gathering of Muslim and Christian Leaders, 2003.

20 Ahmad, *Murder in the Name of Allah*, pp 93ff.

21 Bat Ye'or, *The Dhimmi: Jews and Christians Under Islam*, London and Toronto, Associated University Presses, 1985, pp 201f.

22 Colin Chapman, *Islam and the West*, pp 32f and passim.

23 In addition to the above, see also Bat Ye'or, *Islam and Dhimmitude: Where Civilisations Collide*, Lancaster, Gazelle, 2002; Bat Ye'or, David Littman and Miriam Kochan, *The Decline of Eastern Christianity Under Islam*, London, Associated University Presses, 1996.

24 'Alī Kūfī, *The Chachnāmah* (Mirza Kalichbeg, trans.), Lahore, Vanguard, 1985, pp vif.

25 Bat Ye'or, *The Dhimmi: Jews and Christians Under Islam*, pp 49, 65; Chapman, *Islam and the West*, pp 31ff.

26 Michael Nazir-Ali, *Conviction and Conflict: Islam, Christianity and World Order*, London and New York, Continuum, 2006, pp 87f; Kenneth Cragg, *The Arab Christian: A History in the Middle East*, pp 145f.

27 The constitution is reproduced in A Guillaume's translation of Ibn Ishāq's *Sīrat Rasūl Allāh (The Life of Muhammad)*, Oxford, OUP, 1955, pp 231f. See also Nazir-Ali, *Conviction and Conflict*, pp 61f.

28 See, for example, *The Elimination of Interest from the Economy*, Report of the

Council of Islamic Ideology, Islamabad, CII, 1980; and Patrick Sookhdeo, *Understanding Sharī'a Finance*, McLean, VA, Isaac, 2008.

29 See A. Meleagrou-Hitchens, *Banking on Allah*, Standpoint, July/August 2009, No. 14, pp 51f.

30 See further, *The Development of Islamic Finance in the UK*, London, H. M. Treasury, 2008.

31 See SITC Review, Zurich, August 2006, No. 23, pp 14ff.

32 On much of this, see Sookhdeo, *Understanding Sharī'a Finance*, pp 18f.

33 See further Nazir-Ali, *Islam: A Christian's Perspective*, pp 102ff; *Conviction and Conflict*, pp 155ff; *The Cambridge History of Islam* (P. M. Holt, Ann Lambton and B. Lewis, eds), Cambridge, CUP, 1970, Vol. 2A, pp 82ff.

34 See Gilles Kepel, *Jihad: The Trail of Political Islam*, London and New York, I. B. Tauris, 2002.

35 Cambridge History of Islam, p. 87.

36 M. Iqbal, *Islam as a Moral and Political Ideal*, in S. A. Vahid, *Thoughts and Reflections of Iqbal*, Lahore, Ashraf, 1964, pp 51f.

37 See further Iqbal, *The Reconstruction of Religious Thought in Islam*, pp 169ff; and Tariq Ramadan, *Islamic Views of the Collective*, in Michael Ipgrave (ed.), *Building a Better Bridge: Muslims, Christians and the Common Good*, Washington, Georgetown University Press, 2008, pp 73ff.

Chapter 9

1 Bishop Samuel Wilberforce (1805–1973), Bishop of Oxford and then of Winchester.

2 James Hannam, *God's Philosophers*, London, Icon, 2009.

3 Randal Keynes, *Darwin , His Daughter and Human Evolution*, Riverhead Books, New York, 2001.

4 Adrian Desmond and James Moore, *Darwin's Sacred Cause: Race, Slavery and the Quest for Human Origins*, London, Allen Lane, 2009.

Chapter 12

1 Mary Warnock, *Dishonest to God*: on keeping religion out of politics, Continuum, London, 2010.

2 *Human Cloning and Human Dignity*: The Report of the President's Council on Bioethics, Public Affairs, New York, 2002.

Chapter 13

1 See further Catherine Glass and David Abbott, *Share the Inheritance,* Inheritance Press, Shawford, Hants 2010 and George Weigel, *The Cube and the Cathedral,* Basic Books, New York, 2005.

2 John Polkinghorne, *Science and Creation*: the search for understanding, London, SPCK, 1988 and *One World*: the interaction of science and theology, London, SPCK, 1986.

3 See Thomas Cahill, *The Gifts of the Jews*: How a tribe of desert nomads changed the way everyone thinks and feels, Lion, Oxford, 1998, pp 128ff, 250f.

4 Peter Hitchens, *The Rage against God*, Continuum, London, 2010.

Chapter 15

1 On this debate see Nigel Biggar, *Aiming to Kill*: The Ethics of Suicide and Euthanasia, London, DLT, 2004.

2 See Martin E. Marty, *When Faiths Collide*, Blackwell, Oxford, 2005.

Chapter 18

1 On this see John Witte Jr and Frank S. Alexander, *Christianity and Law*, Cambridge, CUP, 1999.

2   J. Moorman, *A History of the Church of England*, Harrisfield, PA, Morehouse, 2003; and Stephen Neill, *Anglicanism*, 4th edn, London, Mowbray, 1993.

3   James Hannam, *God's Philosophers: How the Mediaeval World Laid the Foundations of Modern Science*, London, Icon, 2009.

4   C. Glass and D. Abbott, *Share the Inheritance: Gifts of Intangible and Tangible Wealth*, Shawford, Hants, Inheritance Press, 2010.

5   See further W. Duncan Reekie, *Spiritual Capital, Natural Law and the Secular Market Place*, London, Civitas, 2007; and Philip Booth (with others), *Catholic Social Teaching and the Market Economy*, London, IEA, 2007.

BIBLE REFERENCES

QUR'AN REFERENCES

ACKNOWLEDGEMENTS

Chapters 1, 7, 11 and 13 were first published by Standpoint magazine in June 2008, January 2010, December 2010 and November 2010.

Chapter 5 was first published as 'Islamic Law, Fundamental Freedoms, and Social Cohesion: Retrospect and Prospect' in *Shari'a in the West*, edited by Andar, Rex & Aroney, Nicholas (2010). Reprinted by permission of Oxford University Press.

Chapter 14 was first published as 'Face to Faith' in the Guardian in May 2010. Copyright Guardian News and Media Ltd 2010.

The author and publishers are grateful to these publications, as well as to The Daily Telegraph, The Sunday Telegraph, The Times, Idea, and Anvil for permission to reproduce their material.

INDEX